ALMOST
PERFEKT

British freelance journalist David Crouch moved to Sweden in 2013, settling in Gothenburg on the west coast. Previously, he was a news editor at the *Financial Times* in London. Now reporting mainly for the *Guardian*, he also teaches investigative journalism at Gothenburg University. In a previous life, he acquired a D.Phil. in sociology. In another previous life, he was a translator and editor in Moscow.

ALMOST PERFEKT

How Sweden Works
and What We Can
Learn From It

David Crouch

BLINK
bringing you closer

Published by Blink Publishing
2.25, The Plaza,
535 Kings Road,
Chelsea Harbour,
London, SW10 0SZ

www.blinkpublishing.co.uk

facebook.com/blinkpublishing
twitter.com/blinkpublishing

Trade paperback – 9781788701563
Ebook – 9781788701556

A CIP catalogue of this book is available from the British Library.

Typeset by seagulls.net
Printed and bound in Great Britain by Clays Ltd, Elcograf S.p.A.

1 3 5 7 9 10 8 6 4 2

Blink Publishing is an imprint of Bonnier Books UK
www.bonnierbooks.co.uk

To Annika

Contents

PART 4: THE LONG-TERM

PART 5: FAMILY

PART 6: IMMIGRATION

PART 7: THE MIDDLE WAY

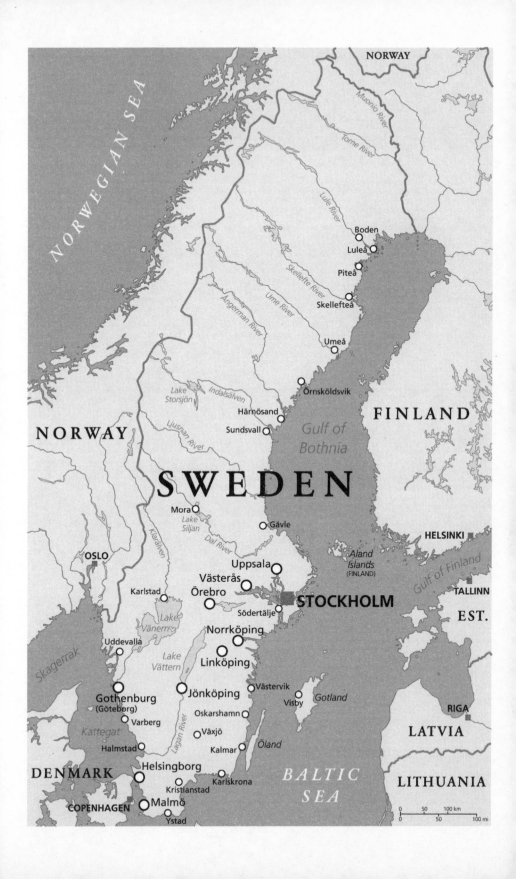

PART 1

WHY SWEDEN?

Introduction
Famous for Six Hours

In the late summer of 2015, I started a rumour that went around the world and reinforced the prejudices about Scandinavia held by tens of millions of people.

It began with the best of intentions. I was still new to Sweden, where I had followed my wife-to-be and started a new life as a freelance reporter after some comfortable desk jobs in the London media. Now I believed I had discovered a good story, so on a sunny August morning I set off to investigate.

My friend Daniel, a photojournalist and outdoors enthusiast, picked me up in his red Volvo estate, normally full of mountain bikes, surfboards or rock-climbing equipment. We drove across the Älvsborg suspension bridge at the mouth of the Göta river as the sun shone on its playful, eggshell green girders. Towards the horizon, a line of vast wind turbines revolved slowly, perched among dark knuckles of rock where the granite coast crumbles into the sea. This was Gothenburg, Sweden's second city and now my home.

We pulled up on a leafy cul-de-sac among the tall birches that surround Svartedalen retirement home, a red brick block in an area better known for its poverty and gang violence. I got out my notepad and Daniel his camera. This unlikely setting was an experiment in the future of work. For the past six months, the elderly care nurses had been working a six-hour day, instead of the usual eight, for the same wage.

Since the 1990s, Svartedalen had been facing more work with fewer and fewer staff. 'We can't do it any more,' Ann-Charlotte Dahlbom Larsson, who ran the home, told us. 'There is a lot of illness and depression among staff in the care sector because of exhaustion, the lack of balance between work and life is not good for anyone.' Already, she said, on the six-hour day staff were feeling noticeably better, but the standard of care had also improved. The new arrangement was likely to be more expensive – the home had hired extra nurses to cover the gaps left by the shorter working hours.

Lise-Lotte Pettersson, an assistant nurse, showed us around, taking a moment along the way to dance tenderly with an elderly man. Caring for the residents, some of whom had dementia, demanded constant vigilance and creativity, and with a six-hour day Lise-Lotte could sustain a higher standard of care, she said: 'I used to be exhausted all the time, I would come home from work and pass out on the sofa. But not now. I am much more alert: I have much more energy for my work, and also for family life.'

I first learned about this experiment from a political flyer stuck to the wall of a tram stop near our flat. The country was preparing for an election, and with the help of Google Translate I was trying to understand what was going on. A bleak and soulless street corner opposite the cemetery, with its injunction to 'Think about Death' inscribed over the gates, seemed like a dismal place for a declaration about the future of humanity. But there it was: something called the Left Party, whoever they were, wanted a six-hour working day. I wanted to be on a beach in the Bahamas, but there was about an equal chance of either of those things happening, I thought. And I got on the tram.

But somehow, here in this wet and windy city on the northern edge of the planet, the idea found a hearing. Gothenburg city council, run by the centre-left Social Democrats who have dominated Swedish politics since the 1930s, agreed to a small experiment at the nursing home. Meanwhile, on the other side of the city, a Toyota servicing centre had moved to a six-hour day more than a decade before, leading to lower staff turnover, more efficient use of the machines and lower capital costs. I trawled the web and found a couple of small businesses that were also using a shorter working day – and bingo! – I had a story.

Sweden itself was about to turn into a much more urgent international story, as the country opened its doors during the coming months to 163,000 refugees from the wars in Asia, Africa and the Middle East. But as for my little story about shorter working hours, the genie was out of the bottle. It turned out that my feature about Lise-Lotte and some Toyota mechanics appealed to every prejudice that we hold about

Sweden, the land of Abba and IKEA, of blonde hair and blue eyes, of sex and socialism and Scandi silliness. Scotland was the first to take notice. *The Herald* wrote:

> What have these wacky Scandinavians been up to now? I will tell you what: experimenting with a six-hour working day, that's what. A typical Britisher will think: 'Six-hour working day? That's immoral. First, it was pornography. Now this. The Scandinavians need reining in.' ... We cannot believe everything they do in Scandinavia is good and everything we do is bad, despite all the evidence. But it's nice to have a beacon of hope, however illusory. And the thought that somebody somewhere is trying to organise society on sane lines gives us courage to carry on in Barmy Britannia.

During the Cold War, the idea that things could be different, that society could be organised along alternative lines, was often connected to Russia. But after the Soviet monolith collapsed and Putin reigned over a regime of ruthless oligarchs, we were left with... Sweden. My story spread like wildfire, to Ireland across Britain, and the US. *The New York Times* even sent a reporter to Gothenburg.

I had gone viral. It hit a breathless peak of nonsense almost exactly a year after my story first appeared, when the website Smart is the New Sexy issued a 40-second Facebook video montage of cheesy Swedish images, actually including a cheese fondue (N.B. that's *Switzerland*, not Sweden), which declared:

'Sweden is officially moving to a six-hour working day.' It was sent to me by an old school friend envious that fate had carried me to this blesséd haven. The last time I looked, that video had been viewed 42 million times.

So what became of the six-hour day in Sweden? As we might have expected, the experiment at Svartedalen came to a close in 2017. Short-term labour costs were up 20 per cent, while the gains were less tangible and quantifiable. The mountain of hype gave birth to a mouse. But the story spoke to our assumptions that in Scandinavia they do things differently, that work might not be just about growing the bottom line, and that a better, richer life might not be just a side effect of the pursuit of profit, but something that can be planned for and worked towards. Could the 'balance' between work and life – a juxtaposition that itself says so much about what work means to most of us – in fact be balanced towards life? And could work, instead of being an end in itself (i.e., the opposite of being out of work) become a means to a fuller life? Productivity in the industrialised world has doubled since the 1970s, so technically we have the potential for a much shorter working day; it's a question of how these productivity gains are distributed.

Like all prejudices, if you look only at the surface of things you can find evidence to back up any theory you like. But perhaps our assumptions about Scandinavia contain a speck of truth around which the pearl of myth has coalesced. I remember my first day at work in the journalism department at the University of Gothenburg. I left my office door ajar. Around 4pm I began to hear calls echoing down the corridor.

Around 6pm I stepped out for a coffee to find the place deserted. The noises had been cries of '*Hej då!*', or goodbye, as staff went home just as I was settling down for a few more hours at my desk, as I had been accustomed to in London. You could be forgiven for thinking this was academia, where the work-life balance might be taken to an extreme. In fact, as I was to find out to my own cost, Swedish universities are tough places to work, with high levels of stress and instability, and staff employed on rolling short-term contracts for years on end. I lost my first job at the university after budget cuts, and I was last in, so first out.

All the same, a working day of 8am to 4pm was observed by most university staff, including an hour for lunch, during which the doors to the building locked automatically, making it physically impossible for students – perish the thought – to disturb tutors during their break. The head of the department at the time also had a strategy of 'management by *fika*', meaning that the twice-daily breaks for coffee and buns, known as *fika* in Swedish, were useful opportunities for staff to share thoughts about their work, and to bond as a team. And it seemed to work. At one of my part-time jobs at a Swedish company, my boss complained that she found it hard to get hold of senior management after 3pm on Fridays because they were already on their boats.

To say anything meaningful about Sweden, however, we need to look below the surface. I wanted to talk to the people at the heart of the country's economy and find out what, if any, are the key features that make it distinctive. For decades, people have referred to a 'Swedish model' of running society, without being too clear about what they mean. I'll try to clarify whether there is indeed a Swedish model in the economy, and, if so, what makes it different from other nations. I will look in some detail at the world of work also, because that is where the Swedish model stands or falls. Work is where the wealth is generated to pay for the shorter hours, the holidays, the parental leave, the welfare benefits, everything that constitutes Swedish society and which contributes to our visions of it – or perhaps, how we would like it to be. When people talk about the short working week in France, it is often in terms of how much damage it does to the economy. So is Sweden different? And if so, how? And why?

The person most responsible for popularising the notion that Sweden is unusual was the American journalist Marquis Childs. Childs came to Sweden in 1933 as a young man, and wrote *Sweden: The Middle Way* (1936). He arrived in the country via a Germany in the grip of the Nazi takeover. To the east, Stalin's forced collectivisation had generated mass starvation, while the Kremlin was preparing itself to unleash itself for the horror of the purges and the Gulag. Meanwhile, his homeland, the US was in the depths of the Great Depression. The horrors of World War II were rapidly approaching, so the notion of a 'middle way' between capitalism and socialism, 'a spectacle of sanity and stability that other nations may study with profit', found a ready audience. Childs wrote: 'It is perhaps this orderly surface of Swedish life that first attracts the visitor who comes from a world in which violent extremes contend for power, in a civilisation that must by comparison seem still amorphous.'

Today, there is a whiff of the 1930s in Europe – the shock-waves from the 2008 financial crash, extremes of wealth and poverty, authoritarianism in the saddle in Moscow, Warsaw and Budapest, war in east Ukraine, and parties on the far-right and left shaking the political establishment. In Washington, Donald Trump has upended all our certainties about the United States, creating a renewed interest in whether capitalism can be done differently, rather than the low tax, small-state solutions favoured by the US president. Sweden itself has seen a radical nationalist party make recent electoral gains, suggesting that the country is not immune to global trends. But it remains a relatively peaceful, open, prosperous country, the economic powerhouse of Scandinavia. This is a book about how people are creating Sweden's wealth – the ultimate guarantor of peace and normality.

Discussions of Sweden tend to be over-politicised. The left in Europe decided 25 years ago that the Swedish model had failed. The main finding of this book is that it has not, but it has changed. On the political right, a generation ago Sweden seemed so closely associated with leftism that it made more sense to scrap all talk of a 'model', rather than trying to reform it. Another finding of this book is that Sweden's reputation as a poster-child for the left is mistaken; many of the model's features appeal strongly to business, and the right has a case for reclaiming it as its own. One should bear in mind that for 13 of the past 28 years (at the time of writing, in 2019), Sweden has been governed by parties of the centre-right. Left and right should take credit – and share blame – for how the new Swedish model looks today.

After moving to Sweden, I spent three happy years as one of *The Guardian*'s go-to reporters for Scandinavia stories, and the paper seemingly couldn't get enough. The *Financial Times* and *The New York Times* also turned to me from time to time. So I covered a hunt for a Russian submarine off Stockholm, women brewers in Gothenburg, the Julian Assange rape case, asylum and immigration, Sweden's wine industry, the property market, moose hunting, the rise of the far-right, terrorism, developments in Finnish teaching and social care, business and politics. I even reported on the Swedish passion for 'drive-in bingo', much loved in the countryside on long summer evenings, where hundreds of people line up their cars in a field while the caller shouts the numbers over a loud speaker.

I came to the subject of Sweden with very few preconceived notions and almost no idea about what I would find. I spent most of the 1990s in Russia – another cold, dark country covered in pine trees. When fate drove me north once more in 2013, at first I couldn't help feeling that I was back in the USSR – more pickled fish and mashed potato, vodka-like inebriants, echelons of apartment blocks and impenetrable forests. It took a while for me to shake off my Russian hangover and see Sweden with clear eyes. The interviews for this book were part of that journey. Most of the time I just tapped the recording icon on my phone and let people speak. Some of my most naive questions – 'So is there a Swedish model then?' – turned out to be the most productive, either because people had different or conflicting answers, or because the issues were so simple and obvious that they had never thought about them properly before. This was a voyage of discovery. Was the country as perfect as envious friends back home in Brexit Britain seemed to think? *Perfekt*, the Swedes would say. Well, almost.

Chapter 1
Almost Different

When Swedish music company Spotify went to New York for the first time to raise money by selling shares, the stock exchange on Wall Street celebrated by hanging out a Swiss flag. The confusion of Sweden with Switzerland is forgivable – they are both small northern nations with Teutonic roots and snow. In any case, what we know about distant countries tends to be based on big brands and historical quirks. Dwight Eisenhower bears some responsibility for residual notions about Sweden. In a speech in 1960, the US president alleged that this 'socialist' nation had high rates of suicide, drunkenness and loose morals – false perceptions that still survive today.

Before we begin our safari into the world of Scandi wealth creation, what do we need to know about this country, its history, politics and values? Is it possible to make any useful generalisations about Swedishness? We all look so similar these days across the developed world: we dress the same, eat the same, work in the same environments, holiday in the same places, read the same books and watch the same TV programmes. The pace of change is fast – what seems to be a stable feature of a nation can soon become an anachronism. So it might be a fool's errand, but it is still fun, and fruitful I think, to explore some big-picture features that make Sweden stand out from the rest.

Let's start with some birdwatching. Each year, tens of thousands of Eurasian cranes gather at the southern tip of a lake two hours' drive from Gothenburg. In early spring you can hear these huge birds calling amid the low cloud, their slender necks stretched out ahead of them. When they reach this lake with its tongue-twisting name, Hornborgasjön, they dance in an elaborate pairing ritual – it is an amazing spectacle. But this is a man-made phenomenon. The lake became a stopping-off point for the cranes on their migration thanks to the potato fields that once formed the basis of the local economy. This used to be vodka country. Potatoes that escaped the harvest and remained in the soil were nourishment for tired birds. The vodka industry has since moved on, so now the locals feed the cranes to keep them coming.

The cranes are here because Sweden once had an alcohol problem, and potatoes were in demand. A century ago, average vodka consumption reached almost a litre a week for every man, woman and child in what was still a very poor, agricultural nation. For decades, the country battled to find a way to regulate consumption. Alcohol today remains a vivid example of Sweden's distinct attitude to market economics, and the ways in which this affects Swedes more generally.

What they came up with was Systembolaget – the System Company, abbreviated to *Systemet*, or 'the System'. This is the state-owned alcohol retail monopoly and the only place where you can buy anything with an alcohol content stronger than 3.5 per cent. The System dominates the sale of alcohol for home consumption, its explicit mission being to reduce the damage to society from alcohol. You have to travel far to find it: there are more golf courses in Sweden (491) than shops where you can buy a bottle of wine over the counter (439). And they close early – at 3pm on a Saturday and remain closed for the rest of the weekend.

The System is a physical representation of Sweden's deep distrust of alcohol in particular, and drugs more generally. It is institutional guilt on a national scale. Entering a System shop is like having sex in church – you cannot avoid a strong feeling that you shouldn't be there. The shops are designed to sell as little alcohol as possible and make no profit. TV advertising plays on this: 'The Swedish way is a little different', a matronly figure admonishes a pushy American consultant who only wants to boost sales. The System's staff claim they are there to help you make the right choice of wine to accompany your food, but no – this is about social control. They are like priests at confession. Forgive me, Father, for I am about to sin. People don't like to be seen with a Systembolaget carrier bag, or to be given away by the clinking of bottles in a public place.

Alcohol shame is deep-rooted. I once went campaigning with a political leader in the run-up to elections, and we needed somewhere warm afterwards for an interview. But she declined to enter a convenient bar in case she might be photographed in a place selling alcohol. In Britain, for example, politicians like to pose with a drink to show they are 'of the people'. This would never happen here. Sweden – a very 21st-century nation renowned for embracing modernity and liberal freedoms – has a significant temperance movement, bigger than most of its political parties. There is no alcohol advertising on television made in Sweden. Ads in printed media are for wine and beer only, and generally just comprise a photo of a bottle and a generic exhortation to 'try this, it's nice'. Each ad comes with a large official health warning informing the reader that alcohol increases the incidence of accidents at work or damages your unborn child. Living here, you would never have any idea that the country supplies the world with that supreme party drink, Absolut Vodka.

I personally don't like the System, it rankles that I am not allowed to make adult choices for myself. And yet, I can reluctantly admit that the tight restrictions on alcohol make sense. This is society stepping in, recognising that unlimited freedom in this sphere has damaging consequences, and saying: 'Let's deal with it'. This is a good principle, at least. And remarkably, the System's popularity is high and growing higher. In 2018, a staggering 77 per cent of Swedes were in favour of the state alcohol monopoly, according to a long-running annual survey. Systembolaget is the most trusted institution in Sweden, ahead of IKEA and Volvo, and far out in front of privatised services such as the railways and postal service.

Social change has chipped away at the System, thanks to internet sales and booze cruises to Denmark or Germany, where alcohol is cheaper and much more freely available. But it survives – and thrives. When Sweden joined the European Union in 1995, it had to negotiate special permission to maintain the monopoly. Until recently there was a similar situation with gambling, so Swedish gaming entrepreneurs were forced to take their businesses offshore. But the internet and 4G have put an end to that. There is a moral panic in Sweden at the time of writing because of a flood of online gambling ads on Swedish television. Perish the thought that the same could ever happen with alcohol.

Booze is also a good example of the conservatism with a small 'c' that runs through much of Swedish society. Marijuana use is ticking up, but it remains far below that of North America or most other European nations. It is illegal to buy sex. This is a highly internationalised country where most people speak English, but national pride is strong – the suburbs are a forest of flagpoles flying the yellow-on-blue national flag. Sweden is often hailed as the most atheist country on earth. But this is belied by the fact that almost 6 million of the population – that's six out of ten Swedes – are members of the Swedish church. Membership is not cheap, it means paying a tax of about 1 per cent of your income to the church. This adds up to billions and makes the Swedish church a very wealthy institution. Membership is down – it used to be more than 95 per cent 50 years ago, and the number of active worshippers is even fewer. But the church continues to hold a respected place in society. One of Sweden's largest active congregations is Katarina Church in Södermalm, the most hipster part of Stockholm. Young people are drawn to the church by all sorts of factors, but least of all by religion, a priest told me.

What about Sweden's famously liberal attitudes to sexual orientation? Sweden is one of the most gay-friendly countries in the world. Gay sex was legalised way back in 1944, while the age of consent was equalised for gay and straight sex in 1972. In the same year, Sweden became the first country in the world to allow transgender people to legally change their sex. Pride celebrations in the big cities attract tens of thousands of people. Stockholm boasts the world's first lesbian bishop. Each year the country becomes quite literally obsessed with the campest event on the planet – the Eurovision Song Contest.

However, possibly because things have been legal and official for so long, there isn't quite the liberating sense of freedoms having been won, rather than bestowed from above. Sweden never had a Stonewall moment; there is no Swedish Harvey Milk. It makes me wonder how deep attitudes go. There are few prominent gay figures outside the arts and sport, for example. A few years ago at the opera house in Gothenburg I saw *La Cage aux Folles*, the musical about gay love, with its wonderful anthem 'I am what I am'. It finished with the well-dressed, middle-class audience clapping politely as if they felt it was the right thing to do. In London, it would have ended with an explosion of tears, hugging and cheering. One gets a similar feeling about official anti-racism in Sweden – it's all very right on, but when you scratch the surface it's not hard to find prejudice, as we shall see later on.

If Swedish values are generally conservative with a small 'c', how does this square with the country's allegedly left-wing past? It is true that the Social Democratic Workers' Party has been Sweden's largest political organisation since 1921, dominating government almost uninterruptedly until the early 1990s. As we shall see later, the Social Democrats reigned during a period when Swedish capitalism was extremely successful. It is easier to fund welfare and income distribution when the tax receipts are rolling in. Sweden stayed out of both World Wars, avoiding the economic destruction they wrought. And, notoriously, it traded with both sides in each of them. Sweden's copper made great bullet casings, and its iron ore made Nazi steel. Neutrality was good business.

Ever since 1944, the Social Democrats' constitution has been steadily watered down. Now 'socialism' gets only a single mention, and narrowly in terms of democracy and equal rights. Since the millennium, the party's share of the popular vote has been in sharp decline. Currently it survives in government thanks only to the tolerance of the liberals. In its heyday, its leftism was largely rhetorical and confined to the international stage – the party's aristocratic leader Olof Palme took a stand against the Vietnam war, nuclear weapons and apartheid South Africa, but also against repressive regimes in Eastern Europe; the Sweden of Palme's Social Democrats was characterised by strong anti-Russian sentiment. At home, for several decades the party presided over a eugenics programme of forced sterilisations, which started out as an experiment in racial biology but later aimed to weed out social problems.

Until 2012, transgender people requesting a sex change were required to undergo sterilisation.

When Palme was gunned down in Stockholm by an unknown assailant in 1986, his murder shattered any illusions about the country being a tranquil haven of equality and human rights, and more or less marked the end of the old Sweden that Palme had come to epitomise. He left behind a country with particularly high marginal tax rates on the rich – above 80 per cent – a relatively high level of public ownership in the economy, and high government spending. Sweden is very different today. Public spending as a percentage of the economy fell from about two-thirds in the mid-1990s to under half today. In the 1990s, Sweden privatised its railways, the postal service, domestic aviation and telephones. Television was deregulated, and private companies were allowed into the welfare sector, while competition was introduced into public services. At the time Palme was assassinated, in 1986, the state employed around 45 per cent of the workforce; today, public-sector employment is below 30 per cent.

Taxes have been slashed and tax revenue is down to around 44 per cent of the economy – still high in terms of the average for developed countries, but much closer to the norm. And most people don't grumble about paying it. On the contrary, it seems Swedes imbibe with their mother's milk the notion that taxes are good because they get what they pay for in terms of public services. Complete strangers will tell you they are happy to pay their taxes. There is a small culture of tax evasion, but it is marginal.

As a result of at least some, if not all, of these changes, Sweden's economy has hit something of a sweet spot in recent years. 'Sweden beats other countries at just about everything,' the World Economic Forum declared in 2017. The country ranked number one in Forbes' annual list of the Best Countries for Business. It was high on the Global Competitiveness Index, and top of the Global Sustainable Competitiveness Index. On the Global Gender Gap Index it took fourth place. Sweden had a very low level of corruption and ranked fourth in Transparency International's Corruption Perceptions Index. The European Innovation Scoreboard put Sweden top. It was third in the Global AgeWatch Index of quality of life for older people. And in 2016 it had the best reputation in the world, according to Country RepTrak Index. When you take out the long holidays that Swedes enjoy, their productivity compares well to that of the United States.

I could go on, but it gets a bit repetitive. In short, we have all heard good things about Sweden. So this is the right point at which to end these introductory canapés and get stuck into the main course.

PART 2

WORK

Chapter 2
Unions

Soon after I arrived in Gothenburg in the late summer of 2013, a garbage truck pulled up at the kerb in front of me. The door swung open and down stepped a tall blonde woman. Wearing the grey overalls of the garbage company, she reached into the bin at the side of the road and slung its contents deftly into the back of the truck. I was dumbfounded. Try as I might, I could not avoid the fleeting thought that here was proof that everything I had ever heard about Sweden was true – a land of blondes and gender equality.

But it doesn't take much digging to demonstrate that flaxen-haired women are the exception among manual workers, rather than the rule. In fact, Sweden has a highly divided jobs market, with women concentrated in certain jobs. Rubbish collection is not one of them. As for the blondeness, nobody has studied this with any degree of seriousness for a long time. I recommend simply walking through a crowded commuter train and trying to count the yellow-haired people – you won't see very many. Or talk to my hairdresser, Matilda, who spends half of her life dyeing Swedes blonde. They typically have mousey hair, she says – or 'rat-coloured', to use the Swedish expression. Not so glamorous after all. This was also the conclusion of a survey of 43,000 young Swedish men in 1926, which found that nearly two-thirds of them had 'light brown' hair, and only 6.9 per cent were blonde ('flaxen'). Swedes today are even less blonde than they were almost 100 years ago.

And yet, to British eyes, there *is* something different about Sweden, particularly when it concerns the world of work. At the airport in Stockholm, before I had immigrated full-time, I had some problems with my luggage. The woman who came to sort me out looked me in the eye, spoke excellent English, and cut through my petty frustrations with a quiet confidence, a light touch and a certain pleasure in her work. This was far from the flustered ignorance, reluctance or 'not my problem' response I had come to expect in customer service situations elsewhere, especially in busy airports. And it is something I have encountered more than once in Sweden – people in jobs that might be considered 'menial' in my home country behaving with poise, professionalism and pride. Shop assistants, waiters, ticket collectors, civil servants, electricians, bus drivers, gardeners – the sorts of ordinary people doing essential jobs with whom one interacts on a weekly basis – usually demand respect, and give it back in return.

Hotel staff are likely to look bewildered if you offer them a tip for carrying your bags: there is usually a career structure in hotels, which is how staff aspire to advance at work through achieving the requisite training and qualifications. On restaurant bills, a service charge has not been itemised since the early 1990s, after unions signed an agreement with employers to regulate salaries across the industry. So your waiter is unlikely to be on a minimum wage, has probably undergone formal and sometimes prolonged training at a specialist vocational college, and has a sense of fulfilment and faith in the future. She doesn't necessarily want a tip, let alone expect it, because of the attendant implication that her living is dependent on your caprice and her deference, rather than on the right to receive a decent wage for performing a necessary service.

It's easy to put a rose-tinted gloss on all this. But Sweden's egalitarian past and its surviving consensus approach to industrial relations have left subtle marks on society, most notably around the workplace. The unions are a force. While total membership has been drifting downwards, seven out of every ten Swedish adults are members of a union – twice as many as in Italy, four times as many as in Germany, and almost ten times more than France, the byword for industrial strife in Europe.

Employers who snub the unions can get into trouble. When swanky Stockholm restaurant Frantzén became the first in Sweden to be awarded a third Michelin star, early in 2018, the public celebrations were followed by uproar – it was revealed that Frantzén hadn't recognised the restaurant union. The irony was obvious. Here was an eatery owned by one of Sweden's richest women, whose customers wouldn't bat an eyelid during a single visit to spend a sum that was more than a week's wages for most workers, and yet the owners wouldn't play ball with the people who represent their chefs. It was shameful that Frantzén didn't want to take responsibility for its staff and for standards in the industry as a whole, the Hotel and Restaurant Workers' Union declared. 'Other companies in the sector will think that if Frantzén lacks a collective agreement, they don't need one either. And then we will lose the entire Swedish model, and all the opportunities to develop the industry in a positive way,' the union said.

Most of the hotel and restaurant industry is covered by union agreements. As if to prove its point, the union has produced a mobile phone app that enables you instantly to check which cafés and restaurants in Stockholm are unionised. As you wander through the city, *Schysta Villkor* – Fair Conditions – can help you choose somewhere to eat or drink at the same time as supporting 'better conditions for workers'. It's even a selling point for employers: being able to say 'we have a collective agreement with the unions' may be attractive to jobseekers too. Collective agreements regulate salaries but also a number of other conditions of employment, such as vacations, top-ups to the state's social insurance, severance periods and support during redundancy.

The trade unions are one of several aspects of Sweden's economy that, from a hard-nosed economic point of view, perhaps ought not to work – the generous welfare system, the high average wages, the improbably long parental leave, to name a few. And yet they do. A former prime minister of Sweden once said: 'Think of a bumblebee. With its overly heavy body and little wings, it should not be able to fly – but it does. ... This is how so-called analysts view the Swedish economy. We "defy gravity". We have high taxes and a large public sector, and yet, Sweden reaches new heights.' The unions are the most obvious 'bumble-bee feature' of the Swedish economy. Nine out of ten workers are employed in organisations where there are national agreements between the unions and management. In the public sector, it is ten out of ten. For more than 40 years union leaders have sat on the boards of almost all companies with more than 25 workers, in most cases making up a third of the board. Each year the unions and the employers' confederation negotiate private and public sector pay rises which apply across industry. And the employees themselves appear to be happy enough with all this, as we shall see.

Anders Malmström is 42. He is an American working for Glue, a small tech start-up in the capital. He has an MBA and an impeccable record in business management in the US and the UK. And he is a trade union member. He had never joined a union before, but when he went to work for a start-up it made sense for him to be part of a union both because of the safety net it offers, but also the advice and support, personally and as an employer – many small start-ups are often lacking in the human resources area. 'For me, unions are something asso-ciated with big, old, traditional companies,' he says. 'But they are the ones that need it least, because they have the most job security. Here things can change quickly.'

Malmström is a member of Civilekonomerna, the Swedish Association of Graduates in Business Administration and Economics. He pays about £35 a month for his union member-ship and unemployment insurance, which will cover 80 per cent of his salary up to a pretty high ceiling 'if it all goes south'. The safety net works for Sweden in terms of entrepreneurship, says this father of three, because it gives people a platform to take risks. 'Unions to me are a relic of the past, so it is cool for me to see how they have transformed into something living with the times.'

Relics of the past are exactly the things that strike you when you walk into the Stockholm headquarters of LO, the huge Trade Union Confederation that organises 1.5 million blue-collar workers, or a third of Sweden's workforce. In the small park opposite, there stands a 1950s bronze relief of the founder of Swedish social democracy, Hjalmar Branting, towering over his devoted followers and looking very much like Joseph Stalin. Once inside the building, you are greeted by a similarly over-proportioned figure – a heroic worker, his chiselled torso worthy of a men's fitness magazine, holding tongs that grasp an ingot of red-hot metal. The fresco by Olle Hjortzberg, who seems to have taken time out here from his usual religious imagery, dates from the late 1930s, shortly after the unions acquired the building.

That was the decade when a cornerstone was laid beneath Sweden's economic model. A landmark agreement with the employers, named after the Saltsjöbaden hotel in Stockholm where it was negotiated, launched an era of consensus and collaboration between capital and labour. The Saltsjöbaden agreement, signed on 20 December 1938, provides the basis for Sweden's consensus-driven approach to labour relations and is the 'bedrock' of the Swedish model of capitalism, according to the *Financial Times*. Even today, 80-plus years on, Sweden is characterised by relative industrial peace and a very low level of strikes.

Karl-Petter Thorwaldsson, the boss of LO, bounces with energy, rattling off the positive features of an economic model based on high trade union membership. Since 1991, the wages of the average LO member have gone up a remarkable 60 per cent in real terms, he says, thanks to low inflation and high productivity growth. The trade union ethic has deep roots in Swedish society, Thorwaldsson explains. Most employers gain more by being inside the system than out. 'It gives us an advantage over other countries,' he says. 'If you want to make an investment, the first thing you look at is competitiveness, and whether the workers expect and favour change. Swedish workers are well known for their pragmatism. The second thing you look at is the number of strike days – our model has one of the lowest levels of strikes in the world. The employers know we have the right to strike, but that right is most effective when you don't actually need to use it.'

Average wages in Sweden have indeed risen smoothly and steadily over the past three decades, and by more than almost anywhere in northern Europe except for oil-rich Norway. This good outcome for Swedish workers is an enviable consequence of strong economic growth that in turn is a result of decades of stable relations between management and unions.

In Britain, as I know from personal experience as a union organiser at the *Financial Times*, workers tend to join unions as an insurance policy against bad times, rather than because things are going well at work. A short stroll from LO's imposing headquarters is a building that is home to a slightly different story. This mundane office block is mission control for TCO, the white-collar union federation, whose recent history suggests unions can be essential to a modern workforce even during the good times. The federation has grown by an astonishing 200,000 members in the past ten years – an increase of 18 per cent. As a result, TCO is snapping at the heels of its blue-collar rival, and soon expects to become Sweden's biggest union federation. It boasts 75 per cent membership across white-collar sectors.

The unions that make up TCO have been so successful partly because Sweden's workforce is changing, but also because they changed their approach a decade ago after a membership slump. 'We realised that even though trade unions were very much needed, young people could not identify with the image we portrayed – they would picture a grey-haired man with a flag in his hand demonstrating on the streets,' says Eva Nordmark, head of TCO. Her members generally have a good working life and good job security. They like their jobs and are doing well, but want to do better. So after much thought, the federation changed not what it does but how it communicates, Nordmark says: 'If we as unions only talk about what's wrong and how bad everything is, workers don't recognise it. You cannot just describe working life as bad – you have to see the potential and possibilities, people want to be happy.'

Unionen, the largest union inside the TCO federation, promotes the trinity of *framgång, trygghet och glädje i arbetslivet* – success, security and happiness in working life. 'We want to make our members feel good about going to work; it would be devastating if they didn't enjoy it,' says Marina Åman, the union's leader. The white-collar unions also embraced economic change. Sweden is a better, wealthier country today because the unions are open to structural change, Åman adds. 'We tend to see change as something positive because it drives evolution forward – but we need to take into account the consequences for the individual.'

We can get a flavour of the kind of trade unionism espoused by Nordmark and Åman through the viral videos in English, French and German that TCO has produced in recent years. Using the hashtag #likeaswede, the series set out to sell the Swedish model to young Swedes by marketing it abroad. The tongue-in-cheek videos introduced a character, 'Joe Williams', a US citizen who could afford to live 'like a Swede', with holidays, parental leave, a decent pension and so on. The idea is to show how people in unionised workplaces in Sweden can enjoy the benefits usually available only to the rich in other countries. Recorded in Los Angeles, the first video went viral in North America in January 2014, becoming the second most shared video on YouTube in its first 24 hours and generating some popular memes. Another TCO video, 'Business like a Swede', is set to music, with performers who rap:

> [employer] I treat my employees with love and respect
> We have a collective agreement no one can reject
> We agree on great perks, talk straight and direct
> And the rising pile of money means it's having effect

[employee] We get parental leave, plus the six weeks vay-cay
So that when we get back to work we're on our A-game
Co-decide with the boss on all kinds of shit
And the [company fitness programme] keeps us lookin' fit

Swedish trade unions don't only say no to everything, in contrast to the reputation of their counterparts in other countries. They say yes to free trade, yes to globalisation, yes to digitalisation, yes even to transatlantic trade deals, opposed by unions elsewhere who fear opening up their domestic markets to greater foreign competition. One of the reasons for this attitude to change is Sweden's unique system for helping workers into new jobs, which we will explore in Part 3. 'We are not afraid of structural change because we have this safety system for our members,' Nordmark says:

Our view has never been to protect jobs, but to protect our members. Our focus is on your next job. You don't want to get stuck in a bad job that you don't like or that you're not good at. Productivity is very important to us because we want Sweden to be a wealthy country. So the unions have not protected old, bad jobs – instead we protect our members. We want them to have new, better jobs. It is important that companies are successful, because that is where our members' salaries come from.

Chapter 3
Management

Let's accept for the moment that the collective power of the unions has underpinned wage increases for workers. But how does management see things? In 2017, an expert body set up by Swedish employers surveyed attitudes towards the unions among chief executives. Bosses were positive about the benefits of talking to the unions, particularly the reputation it gave them with their employees. A collective agreement also improved relations with employees and made it easier to set salary levels, they said. They were neutral on whether dealing with the unions reduced their flexibility or entailed higher wages.

Company bosses were also asked if they would maintain agreements in place even if the unions' right to strike was scrapped. A clear majority – 61 per cent – said they would still like to have agreements, while only 15 per cent said no. The result suggests an overwhelmingly positive attitude towards the unions, particularly among big companies. Eight out of ten chief execs of companies with more than 250 employees said they would hold on to union agreements regardless.

What about other aspects of the model, such as workers having a voice on company boards? The very thought would cause sleepless nights for bosses in the United States or Britain. Carl-Peter Forster, a senior German businessman, is well placed to judge. Forster had a career spanning big-name German, US, British and Indian car companies before he joined the board of Volvo Cars in Gothenburg in 2013. For five years he was also chairman of Saab, the Swedish car-maker, before it was devastated by the slump that followed the 2008 global financial crisis.

'I am German, so I think I can talk a little about labour and the unions,' he says in a spacious office in Lindholmen, the high-tech science park that has replaced the docks in the centre of Gothenburg. Swedish labour relations are not the same as the system in Germany, which also allows worker representatives onto company boards, Forster says. But German boards are typically 50:50 workers to management, which can make it difficult to find a compromise on which both sides can agree. In Sweden, while the unions participate at board level, it seems they are neither legally nor formally as strong as in Germany, he says. 'Sweden has found an interesting model of labour participation, in which I am a believer. Labour representatives understand business, the challenges and what makes business successful. So as far as they are participating in that discussion, it makes things inherently better for everybody, and ultimately better for society. In this sense, the Swedish model is clearly an interesting alternative to the German system.'

The labour participation model in Sweden, combined with a culture of consensus, has created a stable business environment that is 'more flexible' than the German system, Forster believes. The unions have a good position in the system, but they still allow industry to come to decisions more easily and with a smaller degree of formal compromise than in Germany. The culture is 'massively consensual' while allowing people to have robustly different opinions. This Swedish way of behaving is combined with weak hierarchies. 'This is quite amazing, I have never seen a country that is less hierarchical,' Forster says. This all combines to generate informed labour representatives, 'which you do not have in Britain and you absolutely don't have in the US', and avoids the pitfalls of France and Spain, where unions are outside management, very confrontational and 'do not understand the challenges of industry and business'.

At the highest levels of Swedish management there appears to be an almost embarrassed acceptance of the system of strong unions. Industry in the 1970s used to be very sceptical of having unions on company boards, says Leif Johansson, former Volvo chief executive and now chairman of the Anglo-Swedish pharmaceutical powerhouse AstraZeneca. 'My father thought it would not go well – but in fact it has worked,' he says. 'If you sit around the table for 20 years, over time you get a shared understanding of what needs to be done.' In France, often the unions don't trust a single thing that management says, while the Swedish unions have become part of the entrepreneurial business model, Johansson adds. 'You build consensus around the table, which makes strikes and lockouts a last resort rather than first resort. It has made it difficult for aggressive employers or unions to do something dramatically different from everyone else.'

Peter Zhang, a Chinese executive who played a key role in Geely's acquisition of Volvo Cars in 2010 (see Chapter 26), and who until 2018 sat on Volvo's board, says he was warned before he came to Sweden about the high wages and the value system, which he refers to as 'Swedish socialism'. But now he is reconciled to them. 'Socialistic aspects of Sweden include the consultation culture, which is quite unique. … People are more used to talking about things and to trying to find a common forum before they commit themselves to actions.' You might argue that this hinders efficiency, but once a decision has been made after this consultation process, once people feel part of it, they have a sense of ownership, Zhang says.

Ronnie Leten, Belgian chairman of Ericsson and former boss of Swedish tool-making company Atlas Copco and electrical-goods maker Electrolux, says the unions have a very good sense of the feeling among workers on the ground, 'better even than the chief executive and managers sometimes', and they bring this insight to company boards. 'Having worked in many countries, I think this is a good model. It has not held us back at Atlas or Electrolux in taking decisions,' Leten says. 'For me this is the modern way of working.' In the companies he leads everyone has degrees, they read newspapers, they are educated, so it's not a matter of the boss knowing better than them. 'This means you have to work in participation – employees want to be part of it and understand why, and when they understand then they work together with you,' Leten says. 'You can call it unions, or you can call it people who want to be involved.'

Several senior executives told me the unions actually made it easier to sack people. If Annika or Sven doesn't fit with your company, you can negotiate with a sensible union representative, not with the workers directly – which makes life easier for management. 'The unions are very reasonable, they are on the company's side,' says Jane Walerud, a successful investor behind companies such as high-tech manufacturer Tobii, and also Klarna, which enables online purchases where you pay after you get the goods. If someone isn't working well, the unions know about it before management, she says. Hans Enocson, outgoing boss of GE in Sweden, makes a similar point: 'It is easier here than in many countries to trim the tree. French and German unions are much more difficult to deal with.'

The unions are particularly useful when it comes to tough decisions like closing a factory, says Håkan Mogren, board member of the Investor group, owned by the powerful Wallenberg family. By informing them from the beginning, you can convince them that closing the factory is good for the company as a whole, Mogren says. 'And the unions buy that argument. From this specific point of view, it gives Sweden a competitive advantage.' Indeed, unions sometimes fear that legal requirements of confidentiality mean they are trapped, party to business secrets that they cannot immediately share with the workforce, and obliged to take part in painful decisions that they must later defend.

Not everyone is convinced. Consensus can be slow, and at the end of the day, employment rights have to be respected, which ties the hands of management. Keith McLoughlin, from 2011 to 2016 the American chief executive of Electrolux, says he found it 'a little bit shocking at first' when he realised union members sat on company boards in Sweden. As a more consensus-driven culture, things take longer than in the States. 'In the US, the chief executive debates with his team then says: "Here's what we are going to do," so everyone runs out and does it,' McLoughlin says. 'But in Sweden, the response is: "Well, thanks for that input."' He found he had to adjust and learn to convince people one-on-one. But the system works 'fundamentally' because union members start with an assumption that the company's success is in their own best interest:

> When I became chief executive I realised that the nature of the relationship between unions and company leaders is quite different. They start with the premise that says: 'We understand that the company has to make money and provide value for shareholders.' My experience of unions in the US is that they say to management: 'That's your problem, that's what you get paid to deal with, while our issue is to maximise the benefit to our members.' In Sweden at least, unions and management start on the same page. Of course there are disagreements, but the unions come at it from a perspective of asking: 'Is this the correct long-term perspective?' It's a different mindset. You can get a lot more done with a lot less blood, sweat and tears.

Chapter 4
The Future is Flat

As education levels rise and more organisations seek to make use of their employees' intellectual capital, steep hierarchies at the workplace are losing their appeal in many countries. While it is one thing to regard hierarchies as less influential than before, it is quite another to attach a negative value to hierarchical structures, as some Swedish companies have done to great effect. Facing strong unions, a tradition of consensus and a broader culture of egalitarianism, some have made a virtue out of a necessity. Management methods have emerged from Sweden's unusual workplace milieu that may be well suited to modern, complex organisations in which skilled workers produce innovative and sophisticated products and services.

Much academic ink has been spilled trying to establish the existence of a particular Swedish leadership style. According to this work, distinguishing characteristics of Swedish management include a preference for teamwork and cooperation, a non-hierarchical approach, emphasis on consensus and conflict-avoidance, encouragement of autonomy and delegation of authority. A typical Swedish management instruction might therefore be: 'See what you can do about it', rather than a direct order. A collection of interviews with Swedish managers concluded that their leadership style should be seen as a product of the country's egalitarian society, and was likely to be successful in the current era: 'A flat corporate structure is a logical and cost-efficient way to operate, innovate and recruit.'

No other company has made more of its management culture than IKEA – there is more to the Swedishness of an IKEA store than its minimalist products, blue-and-yellow façade and meatballs on the menu. At the heart of 'the IKEA way', the management philosophy first exported to Europe in the 1980s, was a powerful notion that the company was run according to Swedish principles. Managers would be whisked away to the corporate headquarters in Älmhult, the small town in the depths of the southern countryside where the late Ingvar Kamprad founded his empire, to help them absorb the local way of doing things.

Managers were encouraged to learn Swedish if they wanted to make a successful career, according to Anders Moberg, Kamprad's chief executive for 15 years. They would be expected to move to Sweden for a while, living and working in a Swedish environment. 'When we had infused them with the Swedish way, after two or three years we would send them back home and they would be better than the Swedes!' Moberg says. 'They were our future leaders.'

Some aspects of this management style were more obvious than others. Informality was in, so ties were out, says Johan Stenebo, formerly one of Kamprad's most trusted lieutenants and author of a tell-all book about the company. Today it seems like a minor thing, but abandoning ties sent a powerful signal about the company's values. 'In those days it was trail-blazing,' Stenebo says. Similarly, after Sweden in the late 1960s moved to ditch the formal second person plural in favour of the singular pronoun *du*, IKEA did the same in its German stores, branding the shift as the Swedish way. It also did away with titles, so managers and workers referred to each other on a first-name basis. Moberg says: 'People said we were crazy. But it created a very good atmosphere, less distance between management and the people working for us.' They found that people really liked to work in an environment like this, where you could talk to the boss as he was on the shop floor. The organisation was relatively flat, without many levels, he says: you could go to the boss if there was something you didn't like, and relations with staff were very straightforward. 'Many young people grew up with IKEA and spent the rest of their life with us; they felt at home. Lots of people don't feel comfortable in the hierarchical way of being managed, where the boss is God,' Moberg adds.

Kamprad himself summed it up in the penultimate paragraph of his *Testament of a Furniture Dealer*, written in 1976, which became a bible for IKEA managers: 'Humbleness is the key word. Being humble means so much to us in our work and in our leisure. It is even decisive for us as human beings. It means not just consideration and respect for our fellow men and women, but also kindness and generosity. Will-power and strength without humbleness often lead to conflict. Together with humbleness, will-power and strength are your secret weapons for development as an individual and fellow human being.'

In this respect, IKEA was 40 years ahead of Silicon Valley – working for the company was like being at Google or Facebook today, Stenebo says. The attractiveness for Brits or Germans was that Swedishness was something exotic, everyone was on first-name terms and there were lots of symbols of working as a group. 'People bought into it 100 per cent and felt proud,' he says.

Stenebo is sceptical that IKEA still embodies this approach today. His book, *The Truth About IKEA*, while in many ways a tribute to Kamprad, also set out to demolish the idealised image of egalitarianism at IKEA. In reality, Stenebo claimed, it was a secretive dictatorship run with an iron fist by the Kamprad family with help from a network of internal 'spies' who reported on any senior managers displaying signs of disloyalty. Moberg is more positive: the IKEA way is still very much alive, he believes.

Who is right? Here is what American Ginny Figlar, who recently spent five years at IKEA HQ in Älmhult as a copywriter, concluded after her Swedish experience:

At work, people felt more like family than co-workers (and still do). There were no egos. There was no hierarchy. This made working in a corporate environment quite refreshing, but it also meant that decisions were made by committee. In other words, they weren't made very quickly. But everyone worked together, respected each other and had fun. Despite the hard work, people came first. Life came first. You could say the stuff that matters most came first. I've often reflected on my time working there and wondered if what I experienced was because I was living in Sweden or working at IKEA. The line always seemed blurred to me. Was it the Swedish culture or the IKEA culture?

Are IKEA's management methods more widely applied in Swedish business? Tobii is a Swedish high-tech company that develops products for tracking the movement of people's eyes. Walking into the company's offices in Stockholm feels more like entering a university department than the headquarters of a multinational corporation. From behind his large and messy desk, Henrik Eskilsson, founder and chief executive, is eloquent about his leadership philosophy. 'A very hierarchical, top-down structure is effective in organising an army, where one person tells 1,000 people what to do,' he says. 'In a modern economy, the winning system is most likely to be the one that enables 1,000 people in a company to collaborate effectively – without one person telling the other 999 what to do, but rather 1,000 taking initiatives, having ideas, being proactive. You need 1,000 people doing the creative thinking, coming up with innovative ideas. The Swedish culture is well adapted to that, to dare to take decisions and make stuff happen.'

Eskilsson complains that he is treated differently in the US, where employees expected to obey him. When he whispers at the company's Silicon Valley offices, people jump. The Swedish leadership style confuses North Americans – they think it's relaxing, nobody is screaming at them so they can lean back and take it easy. As a result, Tobii has to retrain them, Eskilsson says. In Sweden, however, people are already accustomed to being autonomous and to taking decisions themselves. The hierarchy is there, it is just not so important: 'We want people to understand that we shouldn't let an option win just because it comes from the manager.'

This chimes with my own (limited) experience of working life in Sweden. I also work part-time as the editor of a company intranet for a mid-sized multinational. My manager is been exceptionally trusting. In essence, her approach is: 'I don't mind where or when you do it, just get the job done on time to a high standard and I will be happy – but always tell me when you screw up.' She knows I have a certain set of skills, and she makes sure I am clear about my work goals so she doesn't need to micro-manage me. However, whenever my concentration slips, or big life events get in the way (like writing a book), she steps in to steady the ship. This approach applies to the whole marketing and communications team, and it works very well.

The flat society in Sweden means top management is approachable and receptive, according to Lex Kerssemakers, the Dutch boss of Volvo Cars in the US. 'Some people think it is anarchy,' he says. And sometimes it is – but good ideas can flourish and are not always stopped by middle layers.

'People here are raised to believe that everyone is equal and has the same rights, so they feel they can speak up, they are not hindered by feeling that they can't talk to that person because he is a few levels up. You see that with graduates here. They are very open, sometimes even a little naive, they just talk to you. That means they have been raised in an open environment.'

The Swedish tendency to question authority is perfect for complex software development teams, according to Stina Ehrensvärd, the founder of Yubico, which develops IT security technology. Ehrensvärd moved from Sweden to California in 2011 to build her company. But in the US, her Swedish approach can create confusion, she says:

> Sweden has the flattest organisations in the world; it's okay to question your boss. Nobody can know everything, so I am super-open. I am constantly telling my team they know more than me in their expert areas. In the US people can be confused by this approach. The Swedes question me much more. In the US they are starting to do so, because now they know I'm not going to fire them for it. In countries where you are constantly punished for questioning and doing things that parents, teachers, the state, the emperor says you can't do, people get afraid, they don't want to speak up.

Approaching a senior manager also means sticking your head over the parapet. This might seem to go against another Scandinavian trait, the 'Law of Jante', according to which nobody should stand out or aspire to be above average. In other cultures this is known as 'tall poppy syndrome', from the story of the Roman king Lucius Tarquinius, who was said to have cut the heads off the tallest poppies in his garden as a signal to his son that he should assassinate high achievers to ensure his own success. The Jante law is part of the national consciousness in Sweden, but Swedes themselves cannot agree about its importance. You will hear contradictory arguments: the only Swedes good at sales are the Jante-free ones; understatedness is the key to success, which is why Swedish design is so good; or the start-up scene succeeds in spite of/because of the Jante law.

Jante seems now to be little more than a reminder to the ambitious to be polite to others – rather like political correctness – and with little more significance than that. When groups of people gang up on individuals because they stand out, I think it's more likely due to other factors in society, rather than something peculiarly Swedish.

PART 3

BETWEEN JOBS

Chapter 5
Pain

For Gunilla Stensson life was looking good. She had a steady job as a web developer, living with her daughter in a picturesque village in Bohuslän, the stunning wilderness on Sweden's west coast. Gothenburg was a simple train ride away. A short walk from home was a sandy beach belonging to one of the thousands of lakes that scatter Sweden's glacial landscape. In 20 minutes she could be island-hopping on the archipelago, where the coast slowly dissolves into the limpid waters of the Kattegat.

But then, a new boss at Stensson's work demanded change, and the office moved to Stockholm. For Gunilla, with her daughter at a local school and her life so settled, that meant only one thing – she was out of a job. At first, things seemed rosy. Stensson became self-employed and began dreaming of an independent life with her own business. But then the bad luck began. A job offer seemed less risky and stressful than going freelance. It turned out to be the opposite – the following year she suffered a breakdown. She tried to ease herself back into work with part-time study, but a student grant quickly ran out. Dozens of job applications ended in rejection. And on top of all that, her former husband was no longer sharing their daughter's upbringing.

Four years into her crisis, Stensson found herself alone, aged 47, with no business, no job, no money, and no self-confidence. A support group with other unemployed people only reinforced the doubts she had about herself, namely that she was a single mother living in the sticks who had been out of work for a long time. 'I was really down,' she says. 'I can understand people who think about suicide when they lose their job.' There were so many people looking for jobs in her line of work, and her confidence was low. She felt she hadn't had proper employment for almost five years, and her skills were out of date.

But Stensson had a lifeline. Her original employer subscribed to Trygghetsrådet, or TRR, which loosely translates as the Security Agency. This is a partnership between employers and the unions that provides expert support to workers who have lost their jobs. The agency commits to work for five years with a person to get them back on track. Stensson turned to them and was assigned a counsellor, whom she met every couple of weeks. TRR also paid for a course of psychotherapy. She says: 'I felt all the time that they believed in me, that was the key point. I felt I was worthless. I was not getting any interviews. But they didn't look at that part of me, only at that part of me that *does* have knowledge and skills.'

As soon as she took the decision that she didn't want her own business but wanted a job instead, TRR started guiding her in that direction, but not in an aggressive way: 'It was as if they knew where I was and could support me at each point,' Stensson says. 'Their approach was to actually get this person going again, not just to get rid of them as fast as possible.' When at last she was invited to an interview, TRR arranged coaching over Skype while she was out of town. Her sister-in-law took her to buy a new outfit, and she nailed the job.

Barely a year later, Stensson flashes a confident smile over lunch in Gothenburg, where she is taking a break from her new job. She looks every bit the sassy internet professional, with a job in the healthcare system – she is calm and engaged, able to talk openly about her recent problems without embarrass-ment or self-pity. 'It felt so easy after I went to TRR,' Stensson giggles. 'There was a shift inside me, I found my confidence again – that was the big thing I got from it. I don't know what would have happened without them. It was so important to have someone who kept believing in me.'

Stensson's story is just one among those of the many thou-sands of Swedish workers who find themselves out of a job each year, and who make their way to a job-security agency such as TRR. When Beate Autrum first heard that she was getting laid off from the factory where she worked in 2014, she was mortified – she had moved to Sweden from Germany to work for the company, and she worried about how she would support her daughter as a single parent, and whether she would have to leave Sweden altogether. But she soon found

out about TRR and, like Stensson, was given a personal counsellor to help her transition into a new job. 'I'm so glad that
TRR existed,' she told *The Atlantic* magazine. 'You get this
feeling, of aha, this is not the end of the world. There will be a
chance for me.' Autrum soon found work at another company.

When we think about Sweden's famously generous welfare
state (see Chapter 16), we tend to imagine tax payer-funded
benefits, including those for the unemployed. But job-security
agencies – *trygghetsfonder* in Swedish, known collectively as
the transition system, or *omställningssystem* – are a unique and
largely hidden aspect of the county's welfare set-up, funded
entirely by employers. TRR, one of the largest, is backed by
about 35,000 private sector companies with nearly 1 million
employees, almost a quarter of the workforce.

Companies typically pay 0.3 per cent of their wage bill
each year into the security agencies, of which there are ten.
In good years for the economy, when layoffs are low, money
swells the agencies' coffers as insurance against the bad times.
On average, TRR spends around £2,200 on each person who
turns to it for help, but that figure conceals wide variations
– the agency places no limits on the amount it will spend on
training and counselling to get someone back into work. It
also tops up the unemployment benefit paid out by the state
and trade union unemployment insurance schemes. 'Our
goal,' says TRR, 'is to try and make sure the time from one job
to another should be as short, effective and as meaningful as
possible.' Sweden's system is distinct from Denmark's 'flexicu-
rity' model, which has less employment protection.

The provision of welfare is too often associated with handouts. In Sweden, looking after people during difficult times is a long way from this. The country's transition system, with the job-security agencies at its heart, is an important part of explaining how Sweden's economy maintains its global competitiveness, despite such an apparently well-paid work-force. Helping the unemployed back into work, enabling them to improve their skills or recover from the stresses of redundancy, and making sure they are not penniless during the process has a strict economic rationale. Job-security agencies are good for employers because they make unions more willing to accede to layoffs when competition demands it, according to Carina Lindfelt of the Confederation of Swedish Employers. 'It's easy to have those negotiations, since you know on both sides that these people that will be laid off will get such professional support,' she told *The Atlantic*. Employers feel less guilty about layoffs, too. Sweden's employment minister Ylva Johansson told *The New York Times*: 'In Sweden, if you ask a union leader, "Are you afraid of new technology?", they will answer, "No, I'm afraid of old technology." The jobs disappear, and then we train people for new jobs. We won't protect jobs. But we will protect workers.'

To understand how this unique system – a sort of private welfare state within the welfare state – has come about, we must look briefly at the origins of Sweden's unusual labour market, where the focus is on protecting the individual worker, rather than protecting his or her job. This is a story of the rise, fall and improbable rise again of a unique feature of the way Sweden does business.

Chapter 6
Transition

Behind the scenes, two Swedes helped to shape the country's economy during the post-War decades. In the early 1950s, Gösta Rehn and Rudolf Meidner were researchers at LO, the blue-collar union federation we met in Chapter 2. They had learned their craft in Stockholm as pupils of Gunnar Myrdal, who went on to win a Nobel Prize for economics in 1974. Both were members of the Social Democratic Party, Rehn on the right – he volunteered to fight the Soviets when they invaded Finland in 1939 – and Meidner somewhere in the mainstream of a party that had long since rejected talk of social revolution. Meidner came from a German Jewish family that had fled the Nazis in 1933; later, his radical ideas about evolutionary roads to social-ism would place him on the far-left of the Social Democrats. Neither man was a self-publicist, preferring to address questions of practical economics in trade union and party newspapers.

The problem Rehn and Meidner tackled was this: how, with labour in short supply, could Sweden's rapidly expanding economy continue to grow without generating an upward spiral of wages and inflation? In 1951, at LO's national congress, they presented their solution, now known – mostly to a narrow circle of economists – as the Rehn–Meidner model.

In a traditional market for labour, employers compete with each other to hire workers, driving up wages in those sectors where profitability, and therefore the ability to pay those wages, is higher. This creates pockets of high and low pay across the economy, and sows strife within the unions as members in one sector see their wages rise while others lag behind. To prevent this from happening, Rehn and Meidner made the following proposal: wages should be set centrally, on the principle that workers doing broadly similar jobs should get roughly the same wages – regardless of a company's ability to pay them. Such a system automatically favours profitable firms for which the wages are affordable, meaning they can invest their profits into further expansion instead of having to fight off wage demands from workers wanting a bigger slice of the pie. Simultaneously, companies – even entire sectors – with low profitability are forced either to raise their game to pay higher wages, or to shut down altogether.

The system is deliberately designed to secure a shift in employment from lower- to higher-productivity enterprises. In this way, Rehn and Meidner argued, the overall productivity of Swedish industry would be boosted, as non-productive industry would have to adapt or die. Companies with low productivity would be denied the lifeline of cutting wages to survive. Moreover, if wage levels were set by those sectors that were competing on world markets, productivity would be driven by global manufacturing standards, ensuring that Swedish companies stayed internationally competitive. At the same time, competitive businesses would generate tax revenues to continue funding a generous welfare state.

Sweden's employers were receptive to this idea. Collective agreements and central coordination of pay increases, they reasoned, would dampen wage pressures arising from competition for workers and local trade union militancy. The country's export-oriented corporations already faced fierce competition from their global counterparts, so they had to keep their wage costs below the level dictated by the domestic market. To be able to do this, they needed to control the process of wage formation. Since their famous truce of 1938, union and business leaders had established a degree of mutual trust, which would be essential for a wages system such as that proposed by Rehn and Meidner. Even more attractive to business was that unions would agree not to launch any strikes once pay negotiations were concluded, which meant industrial peace was hardwired into the model.

Workers, however, would need to accept losing their jobs as global market forces drove Swedish industry to constantly restructure itself. To sugar this pill, the Social Democratic government agreed to generous unemployment benefits and 'active' labour-market policies, helping workers between jobs to retrain and reskill themselves to enter expanding, profitable sectors. The traditional trade union demand for job security was replaced by *security of transition* into new jobs. The system therefore encouraged rationalisation and efficiency, but demanded public investment in education and training in return.

This unusual aspect of the Swedish model is almost tailor-made to accommodate the 'creative destruction' that liberal economists describe as the fundamental dynamic of capitalism, believes Thomas Carlén, a descendant of Rehn and Meidner at the economics research department of LO. 'Because the Nordic model is focused on managing labour transitions,' he says, 'security lies in the notion of employability, rather than in the protection of existing jobs. The model is designed to facilitate restructuring. The state, unions and employers ensure that there are measures available to support displaced workers in finding new jobs.'

Some unusual consequences followed from this. First, the Swedish trade unions became pro-market and pro-globalisation. They saw the value of milking the capitalist cow rather than trying to slaughter it, but decided that they had to keep it healthy to get the most milk. Consequently, there were many examples in the 1960s of union representatives at both national and local level agreeing to job losses in stagnating low-wage industries such as textiles, where they would refer to the need for a mobile workforce and structural change. To this day, LO says it regards globalisation, structural transformation, technical advances and openness to the world as 'opportunities rather than threats', and it backs free trade instead of protectionism.

This attitude has taken root in Swedish society. In an official EU survey in 2017, 86 per cent of Swedes – the highest among all EU countries – agreed with the statement that 'global-isation is an opportunity for economic growth', compared to an EU average of 62 per cent. Regarding automation and new technology, 80 per cent of Swedes expressed positive views about robots and artificial intelligence, according to a recent survey by the European Commission. By contrast, a survey by the Pew Research Center found that more than 70 per cent of Americans were worried about a future in which robots and computers carry out work in place of humans.

The Rehn–Meidner framework also created a powerful moral climate that discouraged workers from sitting back and enjoying their unemployment benefits. Payment of compensa-tion was often conditional on accepting job offers or retraining schemes, and it came to be seen as verging on the criminal not to relocate and take jobs in other cities. There was a ruthless pragmatism behind the encouragement of the workforce to move to where it was needed. 'There was a lot of pressure on the unemployed, precisely because we had these training programmes, which essentially forced people to move to other cities to get work,' says Johannes Lindvall, professor of polit-ical science at Lund University. 'It is a mistake to think that the model was a cushy, collectivist system that emphasised only rights and not responsibilities – but there was also a lot of investment when people made the transition to new jobs.'

The system of centralised wage bargaining also gave rise to a remarkably flat society in terms of earned income, with minimal differentials between workers' wages. Wages for the lowest paid were – and still are – higher than the salary that the market wants to pay, while wages for higher-paid workers were similarly lower than a level set by a free market in labour. For this reason, this was known as a policy of 'solidarity wages'. From the early 1960s to the early 1980s, the wage distribution for blue-collar workers was compressed by a whopping 75 per cent, so that a pay rise of 30 per cent was enough to carry a worker from the lowest 10 per cent all the way to the highest.

In a more conventional labour market, this might be seen as destroying incentives for workers to improve their productivity – how can managers encourage their staff without the carrot of financial reward? In sharp contrast with the United States, Sweden showed a weak relation between the value added per worker – their productivity – and their wages. Nevertheless, this unusual set-up seemed to deliver a sharp boost to Sweden's overall economy, at least in its early stages.

Chapter 7
Conflict

The model described in the previous chapter worked well in an economy where many workers were doing similar tasks, which could be measured so their work could be compared. But gradually, under political and economic pressures, the system began to split at the seams. Several factors were at work. The unions were being pulled in different directions. Workers in profitable sectors demanded higher wages, while the left sought to flatten incomes even further by boosting the wages of the lower paid, regardless of what work they did. In the winter of 1969, thousands of miners launched a two-month wildcat strike in the far north, demanding better wages and conditions, which encouraged further strikes elsewhere.

When Swedish industry was hit by the global slowdown in the mid-1970s, divisions arose between employers. Some began to seek a transition away from mass-production methods towards more flexibility, entailing the dissolution of central wage bargaining; others preferred to hold down wages through the central bargaining framework. Throughout the 1970s inflation grew, and wage rises galloped to keep up. Rising costs forced Swedish governments to devalue the currency repeatedly to save the country's international competitiveness, further fuelling inflation and wage hikes.

Meanwhile, a proposal gained momentum that companies should place a portion of their shares under the unions' control, which would increase over time. Employers were furious – these 'wage-earner funds' were seen by business as a dangerous attack on private ownership. Meidner is today remembered much more as a proponent of this radical idea than for his work on the labour market – the battle over wage-earner funds left deep scars. Fuelled by arguments such as this, the consensus between unions and business began to disintegrate.

By the early 1980s, the atmosphere of consensus and collaboration between unions and employers had been replaced by a 'full-blown confrontation regime', wrote Nils Elvander, one of Sweden's foremost labour economists. The relationship that had shaped Swedish industry for 40 years was now in crisis. The engineers' union broke away from central bargaining to strike a separate deal with employers. A few years later, the employers' federation, SAF, closed down its central bargaining unit altogether. Meanwhile, SAF was mobilising against the unions, and in 1983 organised a demonstration of 75,000 people in Stockholm against the wage-earner funds.

Things came to a head in 1990, when the bursting of a debt bubble sparked a deep recession, bankrupting the banks and inflicting the worst economic shock Sweden had experienced since the 1930s. In three years, public debt doubled, unemployment tripled, and the government's deficit increased ten-fold. A newspaper front page showed a picture of a newborn child with the headline: 'Born with a debt of 150,000 Swedish krona'. The country elected its first unashamedly free-market government, determined to put an end to the years of Social Democratic excess. Newspapers and journals across the world proclaimed the end of the Swedish model. In the midst of the crisis, Meidner himself surveyed the wreckage: 'The Swedish system, balancing private owner-ship and social control, has broken down.'

The early 1990s was a period when social democracy was in disarray internationally. In the minds of many, the collapse of the Soviet bloc heralded 'the end of history' and the triumph of liberal capitalism. Governments raced to distance them-selves from what was seen as outdated ideology, replacing state ownership with privatisation while pursing tax cuts and free markets for labour and public services. This transforma-tion was repeated in Sweden, where the Social Democrats were defeated in the polls and then returned to office, but with a programme to continue the deregulation and privati-sation started by the interim Conservative government.

Sweden's business environment started to converge with the rest of Western Europe. Electricity, telephones, railways and the post office were privatised or deregulated, while Sweden's system of vouchers and choice in secondary education became a model for economic liberals across the world. Academics interviewed for this book talked about a demoralisation and even despair among Swedish Social Democrats at the time, who lost faith in classic centre-left policies. Successive Social Democratic governments cut back on the active labour-market policies that had helped maintain skills and ease the transition between jobs.

However, obituaries for the Swedish model were premature. Unions and employers, referred to in Sweden as the 'social partners', had walked away from each other. But behind the scenes, efforts were soon afoot to put Humpty Dumpty together again – despite a global context that emphasised free-market solutions to just about everything. In fact, economic necessity drove them back into each other's arms.

Swedish business was struggling to grow. Employers were failing to curb a new wage-price spiral – in 1995, despite the highest unemployment since the 1930s, strikes broke out and the average salary increase was above the EU average, after the booming forestry industry set a high benchmark for other sectors. This was a watershed year. Major Swedish export companies, which a decade earlier had been the driving force behind destroying the system of centralised wage negotiation, now changed tack. At the same time, the government prodded union leaders to reach out to employers and put their differences aside. The focus had to be on strengthening Sweden's competitiveness, without which there could be no wage rises in the longer term.

A leap of the imagination was required. The resulting agreement between the two sides of Swedish industry, signed in March 1997, lacked inspiration only in its title: the Industry

Agreement. Almost 60 years since the famous Saltsjöbaden deal (see Chapter 2) that set the tone for three decades of industrial peace, employers and unions signed a document on 'industrial development and wage formation' that set out a shared vision for creating a sound economy that could deliver rising living standards. A virtuous circle could be restarted that delivered real-terms wage rises without fuelling inflation or unemployment, while strengthening the competitive position of Swedish industry by developing workers' competence and skills.

In contrast with Saltsjöbaden, widely seen by the outside world as a cornerstone of the Swedish model after the War, the Industry Agreement has no such reputation – and indeed is largely unheard of beyond Sweden. However, the agreement marks not only continuity with 1938, but its rescue and resurrection after two decades of industrial strife. It ended the confrontation regime and ushered in a new era of cooperation. The importance of personal trust built up between leaders of the two sides 'cannot be too strongly emphasised,' Elvander wrote. 'The foundations of mutual personal trust are the same in both cases: the inevitable antagonisms are not swept under the carpet nor unnecessarily blown up out of proportion; areas of common interest are identified, cultivated and widened.'

Meanwhile, the government established an agency, the National Mediation Office, to keep the agreement on the rails. The Mediation Office is a body unique to Sweden; its task is to find solutions that avoid conflict, but within strict limits set by the needs of the country's export-oriented sectors. This new flowering of collaboration means that, 20 years after the ink dried on the agreement, wage norms are set centrally for 90 per cent of the labour market.

The tensions between employers and unions that built up in the 1970s and broke out into a bare-knuckle fight in the 1980s marked an 'extreme crisis' in the Swedish labour market model, says Anders Weihe, chief negotiator for the engineering employers' federation, who has been at the heart of discussions with the unions since 1998. Looking back, he says: 'Did we put Humpty Dumpty back together again? More or less. Our core issue was international competitiveness.'

He continues: 'Collective bargaining is a very effective instrument – if you have knowledgeable people who are not overloaded with ideology, you can create a system where wage formation works.'

This picture described by Weihe could scarcely be more different from the situation prevailing today in the United States, where bargaining between employers and unions is a relatively marginal activity. In my home country, the United Kingdom, there was a fundamental shift in the 1980s away from centralised bargaining arrangements, as Margaret Thatcher led a series of confrontations with the unions. I will leave it to the reader to decide whether these circumstances have benefited either country.

Chapter 8
Belief

When I meet Johan Sandgren, an advisor at the offices of the white-collar TRR job-security agency in central Stockholm, I expect to find him stressed and exhausted – Ericsson, the Swedish telecoms equipment-maker, has recently announced thousands of redundancies, and Sandgren is now responsible for them. Jobless Ericsson workers turned to TRR for help in their droves, two-thirds of them in Stockholm. But Sandgren is serene. 'It is what we do all the time, so we didn't feel that stressed. We had to employ extra counsellors and open more offices, but it is normal for us,' he says.

Ericsson's troubles had seen the company make several rounds of redundancies over the previous decade, so TRR knows what to expect. In 2017–18, many workers took redundancy voluntarily, with a financial package. There was a lot of negativity surrounding the company and many were tired of working there anyway, says Sandgren, who has been addressing meetings of hundreds of Ericsson workers since the redundancies were announced. The jobs market for skilled engineers is favourable, so their prospects are good. 'You can almost feel the difference when you stand on a stage in front of people who are hoping for a new future', Sandgren says.

As we saw earlier, the purpose of Sweden's unusual model of wage bargaining is to maintain the productivity of the economy overall, which in turn requires a well-functioning 'transition system', whereby those who lose their jobs can move quickly into other sectors. With the government's gradual exit from active labour market policy, the job-security agencies have been left to take up the slack.

TRR was established in the mid-1970s when restructuring started to hit white-collar jobs. Unions and employers realised they needed something more than the government-run job centres, which were focused on blue-collar workers and the long-term unemployed. Now almost 98 per cent of all white-collar workers facing redundancy come to TRR. If you are an engineer at Ericsson focusing on telecoms production that has now moved to Asia, you might need some training to take a job in IT, for example. TRR has funds for that. If you are a programmer and you don't have the latest skills, TRR can get them for you. On-the-job training is quite common in big companies, but it rarely has certification – TRR can help with that too.

Then there is the counselling that Gunilla Stensson found so useful (see Chapter 5). When employers handle redundancies badly, it hits people's self-confidence. The combination of a long period at the same employer and shoddy treatment during the transition is a particularly damaging mix: you only know that your competence is good within the company, you don't know your market value, and you are in bad shape to face the future. Sandgren says: 'We get people to feel they have value, a place in the market, to have self-belief. We complement our counselling with a lot of therapy – we know that psychological and physical ill health are growing, and work-related stress is a reason. Companies are downsizing and people are doing more. Also, people are becoming more aware of stress. At TRR people can open up, for the first time they can talk about how they feel.' Like most industrialised countries, Sweden has a fast-growing mental-health problem in the workplace, costing the economy billions every year through lost productivity, social benefits and healthcare. The job-security agencies at least recognise its existence and see counselling as a necessary part of helping people who have lost their jobs.

All the same, when Sandgren visits companies, it is common that half the workers in the audience don't realise they have protection from TRR, and are delighted when they find they are entitled to it. It is a largely hidden part of Sweden's welfare system that people only discover when they are laid off. And because it is away from the public eye, there are few statistics and even fewer studies of how it works.

'Sweden's welfare state today can come out rather poorly in comparisons with other countries, but this system doesn't show up in those studies,' says Lars Walter, associate professor of management at Gothenburg University's Business School, and one of the few academics to have studied the job-security agencies. 'There is no legislation, it is not public policy, but it is really important – it is such a unique phenomenon.' His research on the agencies found they work well, the basic premise is sound, and 80 per cent of laid-off workers are back in a job within a year. But nobody planned it, there is no oversight, and nobody knows exactly what its consequences are for society as a whole. 'It is a system that just happened,' Professor Walters says.

Sweden's transition system has no equivalent in Europe. According to Lennart Hedström, the head of TRR, the transition system is 'lubrication for the labour market'. It is easier to make a person redundant if you know they will get professional support, he believes. Ultimately, the job-security agencies don't create any vacancies. In the event that job creation should dry up, no amount of role-playing or confidence-building will get people back into work. But 45 years since the first agencies were established, the system still works, and works well. 'In the seventies the ideas were totally different,' says TRR's Sandgren. 'But time has shown that this old model still fits, both on an individual and company level. It's a solid part of society. The biggest reason for this to fly is that everyone is happy with it.'

* * *

So what does Swedish business think of a system in which companies cannot pay their workers what they want? For many major industrialists, the gains outweigh the disadvantages. Leif Johansson, the business leader we met in Chapter 3, believes the Industry Agreement was a 'milestone' that has prevented hostile moves by both unions and employers, while ensuring that the competitiveness of Sweden's exporters has not been damaged by high wage settlements in other parts of the economy. 'This is a mechanism in which disputes are handled by independent mediators, it makes strikes and lockouts a last resort,' he says. The institutions of the Industry Agreement have been strong enough to make it difficult for aggressive employers or unions to do something dramatically different. 'It sounds like a rather rosy picture of how wonderful Sweden is,' Johansson continues. 'But when you run a country like this that is exposed, as we are, to international competition, of course there are tensions. However, at a national level we have made it stick.'

For Carl Bennet, billionaire industrialist and investor, the 'special relationship' with the unions is based on an understanding that Swedish industry needs constantly to adapt and change. This is a flexible system that fits the demands of globalisation: 'With that system, we have an attitude towards globalisation that is not negative – people are always questioning changes, but we have a social system that gives the possibility to go from one job to another and have a certain security during this time.' Consequently, Bennet believes, people are not so scared about what might happen to them when they lose their jobs, and they are more prepared to adjust.

High wages also force companies to be innovative, says Stina Ehrensvärd, Swedish-American entrepreneur and founder of high-tech company Yubico: in the US, low wages have not made the country more efficient. Instead, people sit and do really simple tasks.

High salaries have forced us in Sweden to automate, to use technology. That is one of the good side effects of having high salaries – we fully embraced the internet as a way to automate. When we started Yubico we felt like that too, it all had to be automated, this was in our mindset. And because of that we have been able to lower the costs more than if we were manufacturing things in Asia. After the initial investment of robot automation, it provides lower cost at a higher quality.

Another example of this mechanism in action is Stockholm's innovative financial technology, or fintech scene, according to Pär Hedberg, founder of STING (Stockholm Innovation and Growth) a business incubator for some of the capital's most promising start-ups. 'The minimum salary you can pay here is much higher than in other countries, and as a result, many large companies are forced to rationalise and be extremely competitive,' he says. The big banks in Sweden are very cost-effective compared to other countries, because they have been forced to use new technology earlier, which in turn has seen innovative bank employees leave to pursue financial innovations themselves.

Hedberg sees a further positive aspect of Sweden's broader social welfare system – it fosters an entrepreneurial culture. An advantage of having a welfare safety net is that if you fail, you are not forced to lose your home. 'It allows people to dare,' he says.

Niklas Adalberth, co-founder of Klarna, a successful fintech start-up, says Sweden's welfare provision was an additional incentive for him to pursue his entrepreneurial goals as a student, even though he had little experience beyond flipping burgers: 'The worst thing that could happen was maybe I would have a one- or two-year gap in my CV, which no one really cares about.'

Jane Walerud, the investor we met earlier, agrees. If you are an entrepreneur in the US and you have a spouse and children, you need expensive health insurance. If your child has a bike accident, you are in trouble. In the US, entrepreneurs are very young; they need to have no responsibilities. 'Here in Sweden, if someone gets hurt it makes no difference; if the company goes bad, you are still okay,' Walerud says. 'So I get to invest with 40-year-old entrepreneurs who know their stuff, who know their industry. Can you imagine being 40 in the States and doing that?'

Silicon Valley seems oblivious to the value of experience. The average age of entrepreneurs supported by Y-Combinator, a company that invests in thousands of tech start-ups in the valley, is 29. Sweden, by contrast, recognises the cost to society of making 45-year-olds feel as if they can no longer contribute. 'We need to keep people employable and keep their knowledge up to date, because Sweden needs all the engineers we can get,' Walerud says. It is easy to recruit British engineers to work in Sweden, she adds, because the UK doesn't value them like it should.

One consequence of the system's focus on skills and competitiveness is that Sweden has a relatively small share of low-skilled adults, and at the same time a pool of highly skilled people, with a strong participation rate in adult learning. This makes the country better prepared than others to benefit from globalisation, says the Organisation for Economic Cooperation and Development (OECD). Swedish workers have literacy, numeracy and problem-solving skills well above the average, plus some of the highest readiness to learn rates.

However, it is a constant battle to ensure the nation's skill set matches its economic needs. It is not the supply of competent people so much as the supply of the right sort of competencies, says Pontus Braunerhjelm, professor of international business and entrepreneurship at Stockholm's Royal Institute of Technology. Many more Swedes today have university education, for example, but there is an increasing mismatch between the output of the country's universities and the needs of the economy. 'Labour training and retraining – the possibility to be part of a labour-market programme that increases your chances of being employed again – has diminished quite substantially,' Professor Braunerhjelm says.

Let's leave the final word to one of the more remarkable phenomena to have emerged from the resurrected Rehn–Meidner model – the TCO, the huge and fast-growing white-collar trade union we met in Chapter 2. Between 2006 and 2011, Sweden lost 450,000 jobs to automation – roughly 90,000 every year, or 2.5 per cent of the workforce. But the TCO leadership hasn't blinked. Eva Nordmark, the TCO's leader, says:

I am in favour because we have strong social dialogue and strong welfare. Collectively bargained transition support systems mean that if you lose your job you don't have to be poor, and you get support to find new work. The same is true when digitalisation leads to structural change. You shouldn't be marginalised if you lose your job. This is important not just for each of my members, but for the whole of society.

PART 4

THE LONG-TERM

Chapter 9
Jungle Capitalism

In the autumn of 2012, a Canadian delegation arrived in the far north of Sweden to talk about the Arctic. They found themselves in Haparanda, a small town at the northern apex of the leaden, elongated sea that stretches south, separating Scandinavia proper from Finland to the east. They were surprised to find that this remote corner of the planet had not gone unnoticed by history – their hotel boasted that spies, sawmill barons, army officers, noblemen and brothel madams had all enjoyed its hospitality. In 1908, the US explorer Robert Peary purchased furs in the town for the first expedition to reach the North Pole. In April 1917, Lenin arrived in Haparanda by train, taking a sledge over the frozen river into Finland and onwards to lead the revolution in Russia. Thomas Cook, founder of the travel company that still bears his name, declared that a 'true globetrotter' must visit the tomb of Tamerlane in Samarkand, the ancient mosques of Timbuktu, and... Haparanda.

The Canadian visitors were unimpressed, however. 'We were quite sceptical looking around Haparanda, which was a town with no one in the streets,' the delegation's leader reported. At least it had roads, she noted, unlike a lot of northern communities in Canada. Once a busy port, Haparanda's industries such as timber and fishing were 'dying off'. She spied one bright spot among the region's prospects: 'The town is still alive because an IKEA has been built, and it's where all the Russians come across Finland to buy their IKEA products. I'm not sure that putting IKEAs into all northern communities in Canada would have the same success, but you can see that innovation is being used to try to come up with ways to keep a community alive.'

The story of the world's northernmost IKEA sheds a little more light on the way Sweden runs its free-market economy. Naturally it involves the store's founder, Ingvar Kamprad, the recently deceased billionaire, tax exile and folk hero who erected a little piece of Scandinavia in so many households across the globe, in the shape of a self-assembly bookshelf or bathroom storage unit. It was 2003, and the newly elected Social Democratic mayor of Haparanda, Sven-Erik Bucht, was aware of speculation in the newspapers that IKEA wanted to build a store in the far north. The following year, Bucht learned that Kamprad would make a public appearance in the capital, so he flew to Stockholm and buttonholed him. The three-minute encounter between the world's fourth richest man and the left-wing councillor from Haparanda has become legend.

Bucht succeeded in planting the seed of an idea in Kamprad's mind, which somehow took root. It became known as 'Ingvar's project' – building a huge new store in Haparanda, effectively in the middle of nowhere. The entire board of IKEA was firmly against it, Kamprad confessed, because they couldn't see how it could make any money – IKEA stores needed a large population within a certain radius. But Kamprad pressed on. After the opening of the store in 2006, he explained that he and Bucht simply 'fell in love'. 'I am convinced that the decision to build was a business assessment – it was just that others could not see it,' Bucht says today.

In the town itself there was euphoria. One of its oldest residents told a radio station that IKEA was the best thing that had happened to Haparanda in the 90 years he had lived there. The town's economy briefly became the fastest growing in Sweden, house prices soared and unemployment evaporated. Haparanda declared it wanted to become a 'eurocity' where shoppers could use either euros or Swedish crowns, and it was touted as a model for Swedish advocates of eurozone membership. Bucht was named Swede of the Year for halting the region's economic decline.

There was more to Kamprad's thinking than a romantic attachment to Sweden's remote north. His decision to build there was based on similar reasoning behind taking the brand to a handful of depopulated areas in Sweden where he believed a store would have a positive economic effect. 'There must be a helping hand for all the young people who do not thrive so well in the cities, who would rather experience our wonderful nature. We must give them a chance,' he told the press. 'I see it as a social mission – I turn to the many with thin wallets.' About the opposition from IKEA's board, he said in 2005:

> The younger generation is more interested in America or China or Japan or Italy and all that, but I am an old man who thinks we are doing a good job here at home [in Sweden]. … I think the era of old-fashioned capitalism, jungle capitalism, is over and it will be replaced by a modern and responsible market economy that takes a greater degree of social responsibility.

The Kamprad family privately owns IKEA – it keeps its finances to itself, so it is impossible to know whether the investment in Haparanda has paid off. The store claims more than 1.5 million visitors annually from Sweden, Finland, Norway and Russia. But it is not just the younger members of IKEA's board who thought Kamprad was crazy to invest there. 'Of course it is not profitable,' a very senior Swedish investor told me in Stockholm, complaining that the company's private ownership meant it could go against the strict rules of the market without being punished on the stock market. 'Kamprad could do that as a private company. The day he passes away they will sell it,' the investor said, asking not to be named.

Kamprad died in January 2018, and at time of printing the Haparanda store was still going strong. However, the IKEA effect in the town did not appear to be permanent. By 2017 unemployment had climbed back up to 15 per cent, and

Haparanda topped the list of Swedish towns for residents receiving jobless benefits.

The story of the IKEA store in Haparanda begs many questions. Was it just the whim of an old man with more money than sense? Or does it tell us something broader about the relationship between economy and society? Does Sweden really make a priority of 'the people with thin wallets', putting social responsibility above the laws of 'jungle capitalism'? 'History has shown that he was right – it is possible to combine a market economy with a social responsibility,' says Bucht, who went on to become a government minister. Politicians would never deny that people come before profits, but what do Sweden's biggest capitalists say?

Before we search for answers, we must look briefly at a peculiar feature of how Swedish industry is owned and controlled. In international business circles, Sweden has a reputation for encouraging long-term ownership of companies through good times and bad. This stands in contrast to the shorter-term outlook inherent in the so-called 'Anglo-Saxon model' of capitalism, which allegedly emphasises short-term profits at the expense of long-term planning. The Anglo-Saxon approach also combines lower taxes, looser regulation, a weaker social safety net, and greater ease for firms to hire and fire employees. At business level, it puts the interests of shareholders above those of other stakeholders, such as employees.

In Sweden the bulk of the economy is controlled by large investment organisations – some of them owned by powerful families – with a track record of owning and managing companies for decades, so a long-term philosophy is built into their thinking. While the majority of companies listed on the stock exchange in the UK or the US, for example, have a very diverse ownership structure, ownership in Sweden is often concentrated in the hands of a single or small numbers of major shareholders. They often play an active ownership role and take particular responsibility for the company, for example by sitting on the board of directors.

This is further encouraged by an unusual system of 'dual-class' share ownership, also known as A and B shares, which gives some shareholders a bigger stake in running the company if they commit for the longer term. Owners of A shares, which are more expensive, have much more say over how the company is managed, so that even a minority shareholding can mean dominance over a company's long-term direction. In around half of Swedish listed companies, shareholders strengthen their positions by holding A shares that grant them greater voting rights.

This is a Swedish model of 'active ownership', where shareholders are expected to exercise their power over the long term, rather than just looking to bail out if they think management is likely to damage the share price. After the financial crash of 2008, in which short-term, get-rich-quick thinking played a role, this model attracted attention internationally among governments and regulators seeking to avoid another slump.

But does it work? And how has long-term thinking shaped the kind of economy that Sweden has created?

Chapter 10
The 100-Year Plan

In 2011, Keith McLoughlin, a senior US executive, was appointed boss of Electrolux, the giant Swedish maker of washing machines and refrigerators. He wanted to hit the ground running with a plan for his first 100 days – a period for which new governments, presidents and business chiefs are commonly assessed. But for McLoughlin, this would turn out to be a lesson. 'When I was first appointed I thought it would be good to interview every director on the board individually,' he recalls. He met three or four of them, all Swedes, asking for their input on the issues and opportunities, and shared with them the main points of his 100-day plan. But there were puzzled looks and furrowed brows. 'I could tell the interviews were not going well,' McLoughlin says. 'Then this guy said: "I want to give you a tip. For a Swedish director to hear about a 100-day plan makes us very nervous. We want to hear about your 100-*year* plan."'

For the new boss, his colleagues' reaction was unnerving. But he came to see the long-term outlook as a positive feature – instead of judging progress purely in terms of the next quarterly report to the market, which reacts by praising or punishing management's performance through the share price, he could look beyond short-term setbacks in favour of sustainable long-term goals. 'The whole quarterly thing with a publicly traded company doesn't always create the most value for the shareholder,' McLoughlin says. 'The vast majority of shareholders in the US hold shares for under a year. So their time window and horizon gives them a very different perspective from someone who is holding the share for the long term, who wants to be certain that every decision is adding value, someone who doesn't worry about the short-term gyrations. If you hold stock for less than a year it is *all* about the gyrations.'

Richard Twomey, a broad-chested Welshman who has spent decades at the top of big life-science companies, was based in California when he got the call to swap surf and sunshine for the grey skies of Gothenburg. He took over a company with an unpronounceable name that is nonetheless a world leader in manufacturing medical products: Mölnlycke Healthcare. When my mother was being nursed in the last months of her life in a small town on England's south coast, it was dressings made by Mölnlycke Healthcare that helped to heal the frequent tears in her delicate skin – a connection with my new home town that my family discovered only after her death.

Twomey's initial reaction to Scandinavia was not positive, he told the *Financial Times*. 'Sweden, you have got to be joking. Cold and wet, and there's no surf.' For Twomey, a keen surfer, this was a problem. But a determining factor for him was the company's long-term outlook. In Sweden, investors hold on for the long term: 'If you want to be a chief executive, this is a dream environment in which to do it. A big reason I came here was the ownership.'

What is more, Twomey was wrong about the surf. A stretch of sand 30 minutes to the south of Gothenburg delivers reasonable waves after a windy night. When I met him at the company's HQ, Twomey was already anticipating a 5pm getaway for the beach. But first, he found time to explain how the long-term perspective was a 'conservative and very sensible' way to run industry. 'If you've got to sum up Swedish business and industry, that's pretty much what makes it different,' he says. Twomey points to other Swedish corporate giants such as SKF, Volvo and Atlas Copco – all of them very well-run businesses that are managed for the long term. 'There is a certain patience here: it is a dream environment. You put a plan in place and you have complete understanding and alignment with the owners and the board.'

If a company is hit by crisis, the model allows time to address the problem and implement a well-planned transition that is not driven by short-term market considerations, Twomey believes. He sees only one equivalent in the Anglo-Saxon business sphere: the US investment company Berkshire Hathaway, run by US investment guru Warren Buffett, which also seeks to buy good companies, put competent management in place and invest for the long term.

In Sweden, major shareholders don't panic over a quarterly result that isn't up to expectations, according to Stu

Graham, a US executive who spent 26 years (including six as chief executive) at the top of Skanska, the Swedish multinational construction group. 'The long-term owners insist on results, so it is not the case that the set-up takes the heat off management. They hold our feet to the fire,' Graham says. 'But it is a very comforting way of doing business.'

Skanska's main shareholder is an investment company called Industrivärden, while Mölnlycke is controlled by the Wallenbergs' Investor group. Together, these two 'holding companies' – which hold on to the shares of companies, rather than producing goods or services themselves – control more than half the Swedish economy. The overriding aim when buying stakes in companies is 'buy to build, not buy to sell', says Johan Forssell, chief executive of Investor. Investor holds controlling stakes in 18 Swedish companies. 'Our strategy is to work with them and develop them as if we are going to own them for 50 years or longer,' he says, sitting in Investor's ornate offices close to Stockholm's central waterfront.

If Investor wished to make a profit from selling off the company silver, there is no shortage of global companies who would like to buy any one of their holdings. But for Forssell, doing so only creates short-term cash for Investor, rather than long-term value. His reasoning goes like this: when you buy a company, you hope it is a great performer, efficient and profitable, but you need to own it for a number of years before you can really know. If you sell it, you might get a good price, but then you need to buy *another* great company. That would mean paying a high price, but without detailed knowledge of its potential, which only comes after a few years of owner-ship. Lots of companies can look cheap on paper, but often they won't turn out to be a cheap acquisition in ten years' time because they will perform poorly. 'If you pay a high price for a great company, leading the market in an attractive niche, in ten years' time normally it will turn out to have been a great deal,' Forssell says. 'If you invest in a company and you plan to keep it for decades, you have to go for the good ones.'

Like Twomey, Forssell is also a fan of Warren Buffett, who said it is better to buy a wonderful company at a fair price than a fair company at a wonderful price. Industrivärden, the other huge investment house that dominates Swedish business, professes to have the same approach. 'It's important for every company to have one or a few big shareholders who take a long-term view and long-term responsibility,' the group's chief, Fredrik Lundberg, told the *Financial Times*.

The dual-class share model, with more power for owners who commit for the long term, is an 'oddity' that is peculiar to Sweden, says Björn Wahlroos, Finland's leading business-man and chairman of Sweden's largest bank, Nordea. But its importance is waning, he believes, as more and more shares in Swedish companies are owned internationally – currently some 40 per cent of the Stockholm stock exchange. It has had one demonstrable positive effect: Swedish industry has invested more in Sweden. But it is no panacea: 'Is this a good idea? The libertarian in me says be my guest.'

Dual-class shares are not exclusive to Sweden. When Google went public in 2004, its founders, Larry Page and

Sergey Brin, insisted on a dual-class share structure so that, with around one-fifth of Google's total shares, the founders still commanded about three-fifths of the votes, and thus retained control. Google made dual-class shares fashionable again in North America: Facebook's dual-class model gives company founder Mark Zuckerberg less than 1 per cent of the social-media giant's publicly traded stock and 60 per cent of its voting rights. Sweden is merely the European country in which the practice is most widespread: some two-thirds of its stock-market listed companies have them.

The ownership structure of the bulk of Swedish industry is a key element of the Swedish model, according to Mats Andersson, a senior Swedish financier. He points to the fact that the Swedish stock exchange has consistently outper-formed the MSCI World Index by 5 to 7 per cent over the past 20 years. Andersson says he became aware of Sweden's uniqueness when he became the boss of AP4, one of Sweden's big national pension funds. For more than a decade from the mid-2000s, he was responsible for invest-ing Swedes' pension contributions. Under the Anglo-Saxon model of capitalism, he says, ownership is fragmented and shareholders are largely passive, not interested in how managers run the company:

> They leave the work of good governance to others, they are free riders, their only driver is to drive down costs. We all know markets are not perfect, therefore I am an advocate of active management of money. The important

ingredient is to make owners accountable, make sure they are active and responsible. In a world where investors are becoming more short-term oriented, we need more long-term investors.

Chapter 11
Social Responsibility

Some at the top of Swedish industry go further than the long-term perspective. For them, running companies means more than just better business performance – it is also an element of a broader philosophy that stresses the need to spread the benefits from business throughout society, rather than concentrate them among a wealthy few.

On paper, Carl Bennet is one of Sweden's wealthiest men, having successfully invested in Swedish medical technology and the life sciences. He has been on the board of global healthcare equipment-maker Getinge for almost 30 years. From inside a glass-walled eyrie perched high on a vaulting rock above Slottsskogen park in Gothenburg, Bennet cannot get enough of the long term. He complains that Sweden has lost control of some important companies because their owners preferred to sell them off. He himself is approached every year by competitors who want to purchase the companies he controls, but for Bennet it is not about feathering his own nest, but rather 'a life-long journey' to develop these businesses.

'With a long-term perspective you are making sure it will benefit society,' he says. 'With a short-term approach, you get in, do your best, take money and go away; you are stepping into a business in order to abandon it, to make a big profit. You go in to get out. If you are in for the long term, you don't maximise things for the benefit of yourself and a few others.' Short-sighted actions can make society vulnerable, he believes, if you just want to make as much profit as possible, you leave behind a lot of people who question how much you took and what you were thinking about when you took it.

On the contrary, he says, running a business to develop it legitimatises the capitalist system and the market economy. His outlook has earned him a reputation as the 'red baron', a capitalist who leans to the left. Bennet himself rejects the moniker. 'I believe strongly in the market economy. I think we should develop the country and make sure we distribute the wealth in a way that it can benefit many people.'

There is an echo of this approach in the guiding principles of the Wallenberg family's approach to business, which involves the idea of *landsgagneligt*, or 'benefiting the nation'. It feels rather like the old-fashioned attitude of a captain towards his vessel – you are with it to the last, and you would go down with it rather than jump in the lifeboat and abandon ship. Jacob Wallenberg, Sweden's best known industrialist, says the essence of the Swedish model is a balance between fostering capitalism and taking responsibility for people who struggle to fit in. Failure to do this in the US is part of the reason why Donald Trump became president, Wallenberg says.

'There are different ways to run things, one system does not outshine the others. I would argue there is a Swedish or Scandinavian model which is a balance, where on the one hand you try to create the best possible circumstances for economic development – entrepreneurship, innovation, R&D [research and development], where education is fundamental – but also a society with a significant sense of responsibility.'

So-called 'angel investor' Jane Walerud came to Sweden from the US in the early 1980s and married a Swede, so she knows the country closely. She describes herself as a serial entrepreneur and, as previously mentioned, is behind Swedish business successes such as Tobii and Klarna. When I met her at SUP46, a start-up café in central Stockholm, we were surrounded by people half our age. Walerud stood out from the caffeine-fuelled twenty-somethings for her steady gaze, soft voice and calm but forceful presence.

Talking about what makes Sweden different, she starts with the high levels of trust. This means deals can be done on a handshake, which brings down costs, she says, because you don't need so many detailed contracts and lawyers. But a big part of that trust stems from the fact that most people in business believe that others are out for the good of the whole organisation, not just themselves, Walerud says. 'When I do business in the UK, often the reaction from the people I am doing business with is: you want to sell the company straight away, so I'm not going help you. I say no, we are trying to build a company, selling is not the goal. They just don't believe me, because in the UK the general idea is to get as rich as possible as quickly as possible, and not necessarily to contribute to society as a whole.'

Walerud sits on the country's National Innovation Council, chaired by the prime minister. Although she is on the right in political terms, she has been pushing an idea that will give more power to the trade unions. 'That's just me contributing to the society, and everyone expects that I will,' she says. 'We need people to feel that we are looking out for them. We are all coming from the same place, we share the same reference, we agree approximately about where Sweden is. We have different priorities but we still agree to a great extent about the way we want Sweden to develop. This is loyalty to the community because this is where we live.'

Seen in this light, perhaps Ingvar Kamprad's willingness to build an IKEA in Haparanda makes a little more sense. IKEA's Anders Moberg, who we met in Chapter 4, is not scared to use the 'S' word. Kamprad, he says, 'was a capitalist but very much socialist in his way of being and acting. One dimension was business, but there was also a social dimension.' Kamprad's approach seems to have rubbed off on Moberg:

I am a little bit socialist too. You need to take a social responsibility for what you are doing. If we don't pay attention to this we will get a very divided world. The United States is the worst example – it is scary how divided countries are. In the mission of IKEA to sell good design at affordable prices, you already have a very social approach. You can make money on that, but not on every piece you sell. You need to be there for the many in order to do it.

Chapter 12
The Limits of *Lagom*

When wealthy business people start to bang on about the common good – let alone 'socialism' – I find it hard not to raise an eyebrow. How serious is Sweden's capitalist class about redistribution? Is it just putting a self-serving gloss on the successful lining of its own pockets?

The 'we're all in this together', ties-off, first-name-terms approach might help to motivate middle managers, but it surely has its limits. IKEA's Ingvar Kamprad moved to Switzerland in 1973 to avoid paying Swedish taxes, and relocated his company HQ to the Netherlands for the same reason. Kamprad largely got away with it – and his youthful membership of Sweden's Nazi movement – because Swedes basked in IKEA's global glory. Other wealthy Swedes have also jumped ship, such as Hans Rausing, billionaire scion of the Tetra Pak business, who fled the country's high taxes decades ago and moved his corporate HQ to Switzerland.

As we have seen, the long-term approach to investment is hardwired in the Swedish model, but far more important in terms of curbing animal instincts at the top of Swedish business is a national culture in which public figures are subjected to minute scrutiny over their financial affairs. Famously, a former leader of the Social Democrats was forced to take a three-year break from politics in the mid-1990s after it emerged she had used her government credit card to purchase personal items, including bars of Toblerone chocolate. A prosecutor's investigation found Mona Sahlin had broken no rules, but the 'Toblerone affair' effectively prevented her from becoming Sweden's first female prime minister.

Swedish newspapers like nothing more than to question whether wealth is justified by performance. Following the 2017 'Paradise Papers' – the leak of millions of documents about secret offshore accounts – investigative journalists calculated that Sweden loses more than £3.4 billion in tax revenue each year, or about 4 per cent of the government's annual spending – enough to pay the salaries of 100,000 nurses or educate 400,000 children – because of offshore tax avoidance by wealthy Swedes. Leif Östling, head of the Confederation of Swedish Enterprise and a former boss of truck-maker Scania, was forced to quit after it was revealed that he held several million euros in an offshore account, while private care companies relied on taxpayers' money to make their profits.

In response to questions about his taxes, a visibly annoyed Östling blurted out: 'What the hell do I get for my money?', a phrase that began trending on Twitter soon afterwards. Swedes were angry at his assumption that the super-rich have the right to take things into their own hands and buck the system. It offended their sense of *lagom*, that things should be 'in moderation', or 'just enough' – a sort of Goldilocks' philosophy that holds that nothing in society should be too hot or too cold, but just right. It fell to the leader of Sweden's Conservatives to point out to Östling: 'This is not how it works in Sweden, nor is it going to work. You pay taxes on the basis of what you earn, you don't get back more from the state because you pay more taxes.'

Sweden's executives were reminded of the lines they should not cross in 2015 when a scandal swept through some of the country's biggest companies, toppling some major names in one of the biggest shake-ups in Swedish boardroom history. It stemmed from newspaper revelations about corporate perks – namely that SCA, a pulp and paper company which is part of the Industrivärden empire, had flown executives to Formula One races, the World Cup and the Olympics. Attention focused on a lodge built by the company on prime moose-hunting land in a beautiful part of central Sweden, where potential business partners were entertained. Wives, children and pets accompanied directors on these trips.

An internal investigation found that none of the directors broke company policy, and it is hard to imagine executive behaviour of this nature making such big headlines in other countries, or having such a drastic impact. But the details made uncomfortable reading in a nation in which the sinews of social democracy are still more or less intact, despite being stretched and strained by globalisation since the early 1990s.

The scandal also exposed an incestuous system of cross-ownership, in which executives sat on many boards and approved each other's expenses. It led to a major clear-out of chief executives and chairmen as Industrivärden struggled to clean up the mess.

The revelations demonstrated a casual profligacy at the top of a country that feels uncomfortable with extravagance, lifting the lid on a secretive world of corporate perks in a society that has embraced globalisation but is hostile to ostentatious displays of wealth and privilege. Sweden's main business daily called on the country's capitalists to think about their legitimacy in the eyes of the wider population. The paper made a comparison between unelected business executives and Sweden's royal family, whose popularity has also slipped in recent years among a population disturbed that some of its fellow citizens can still be born into privilege: 'A monarch who clearly contributes to the development of society can bridge the gap between a culture of democracy and the right to inherit the throne.' In a country where multiculturalism is celebrated and atheism is the norm, the white, patriarchal, Protestant and unelected institution at the pinnacle of society seems to stand for everything on which Sweden is trying to turn its back.

When, 20 years ago, leaders of Britain's centre-left Labour Party were trying to burnish their credentials with business, one of Prime Minister Tony Blair's leading ideologues famously said the party was 'intensely relaxed about people getting filthy rich'. There isn't a herring's chance in a pickling factory that any Swedish politician could get away with a statement like that, let alone somebody on the left. Sir Michael Marmot, leader of a seminal World Health Organization report on inequality and held up as something of a guru on the subject in Sweden, told me: 'In Sweden even right wing governments do not look so right wing, they broadly have the same commitment to a social democratic model.'

Sweden has not been immune to international trends. There is an obvious tension between the country's traditional egalitarianism and its attempts to create an environment where capitalism, and capitalists, can flourish. The rich have got richer in Sweden, as in many other countries. 'There is a lot of rhetorical agreement on equality, very few politicians would say they are against it because we have such a strong egalitarian tradition here,' says Per Molander, a former adviser to the International Monetary Fund (IMF) and author of a recent history of inequality. 'But there is a large gap between rhetoric and reality. The fact is, the growth in inequality since the 1980s has been the largest among all OECD countries.'

Sweden has long been seen as a paragon of fairness. The centre-left has governed the country for 80 of the past 100 years, for most of which it strived to be the *folkhemmet* – or 'people's home' – in which the state was like a family, caring for all and with no one left behind. By all indicators, Sweden became one of the most socially equal countries in the world. A shift started, however, when the Social Democrats began introducing free-market policies and deregulating the credit market, but change accelerated after the 1990s economic crisis. A booming housing market and stock exchange led to soaring capital income from the sale of property and shares. Senior managers' income has 'decoupled' from the rest, according to economist Thomas Carlén. Sweden now has nearly 200 krona billionaires (one billion Swedish crowns is worth roughly £80 million), a number that has steadily increased over the past decade. Together, Sweden's richest own more than twice the annual budget of the Swedish state, and the number of dollar millionaires is also rising.

A fad among Stockholm's gilded youth in the years after the financial crash was *vaskning* – the ostentatious 'sinking' of bottles of champagne by pouring them down the drain. Instead of buying one bottle you would get two, then ask the barman to pour one of them away. Meanwhile, in 2016 the UN children's agency Unicef reported that Sweden was on a 'downward trajectory' in terms of the life chances available for its poorest children, a growing number of who were 'very disadvantaged'. A Swede with only a basic education can expect to live five years less than a university-educated compatriot, says the country's Public Health Agency. In my home town of Gothenburg, the gap between rich and poor almost quadrupled over two decades. The council survey's most shocking discovery was that people in affluent areas were living nine years longer than those in poor ones. When journalists compared a street of private mansions on the coast with overcrowded apartments occupied mainly by jobless immigrants on the other side of town, they found an income gap of more than half a million krona (£40,000).

By these measures, Sweden comes out clearly as a society of haves and have-nots. However, when capital income is excluded, the gradual increase in inequality since the 1990s is significantly flatter – in other words, wage inequality has not grown so much. Where it has, the causes are fairly straight-forward: tax cuts in some areas and cuts to welfare in others. Also, Sweden still ranks relatively high for social equality compared to other countries in Europe.

The problem of rising inequality is recognised at a national level and there is growing political will to do something about it. There has been a change in the political climate: 'Now all the parties are talking about inequality,' says Olle Lundberg, chair of the recently established Commission for Equity in Health. The three main cities – Stockholm, Gothenburg and Malmö – have set up organisations tasked with investigating the problem and what to do about it. The Equal Gothenburg programme is mobilising the city's resources and promis-ing long-term investment to reduce inequalities, focusing in particular on children's early years. Political opposition to the programme is muted, more about how, rather than whether or why, to do something about it. 'If you increase equality, you get more trust and stronger growth: it's a win-win situation,' the city's left-wing mayor, Ann-Sofie Hermansson, told me. 'It is about decency, but it is also good for the economy.'

Hermansson's suggestion that sustainable growth demands constraints on social inequalities is not a Gothenburg discov-ery, nor even a Swedish one. Some big hitters in the world economy have been pushing this message in recent years. The

IMF, which imposed free-market 'stabilisation programmes' on wayward nations during the 1990s, argues today that reducing inequality can help support durable growth. It goes so far as to suggest that increasing the income share of the poorest can boost an economy, while raising the income share of the richest can actually harm it. The IMF now says that all this puts addressing inequality squarely within its mandate to help countries improve economic performance, and it is researching how countries can tax and spend more effectively.

Rising inequality knocked more than 10 percentage points off growth in Mexico and New Zealand over the past two decades up to the global financial crash, the OECD estimates, while in Italy, the UK and the US the cumulative growth rate would have been six to nine percentage points higher had income disparities not widened. On the other hand, greater equality helped increase GDP per capita in Spain, France and Ireland prior to the crisis. The main mechanism through which inequality affects growth is by undermining education opportunities for children from poor socio-economic backgrounds, lowering social mobility and hampering skills development. It also found no evidence that redistributive policies, such as taxes and welfare benefits, harm economic growth – provided, of course, that these policies are well designed and targeted.

So if Sweden can restore its sense of *lagom* in this sphere, and reverse its trend towards growing inequality, it will not just be reverting to historical type, but also singing in tune with recent economic thinking. Since social changes of this nature take time, they will demand far-sighted politicians looking to the long term, rather than fixating on the next opinion poll. In this respect, the country's social policies would also be more in line with the investment approach of its biggest capitalists, which appear to pay more than lip service to long-term outcomes and recognise the need to spread the benefits of business throughout society.

PART 5

FAMILY

Chapter 13
Freedom

There it is: the thin blue line inside the window of the pregnancy test. After the initial elation, there is a nagging question: how are we going to afford the childcare? I think it's probably fair to say that this is a sensation unknown to most Swedes. It is no secret that, in relative terms, Swedish parents enjoy a significant amount of paid time off work to be with small children, while day-care facilities are heavily subsidised by the state. There might be many questions about how a child will change the way you live your life, but in Sweden 'Can we pay for childcare?' is not one of them.

'This is one of the things that you take for granted when you are born in Sweden,' says Linnéa Mitchell, a yoga instructor in Stockholm. She gave birth to Theo in London in 2010, and to Freja in Stockholm four years later. When Theo came along, Mitchell had already quit her London job. Before the birth, her experience of the taxpayer-funded UK National Health Service (NHS) was very good, and for 18 months Mitchell was happy to be at home with her son – her British husband Phil was making good money. But it was when she wanted to get back into work that the problems began. Soon the family was paying the equivalent of £350 a month for Theo to spend just three mornings a week at nursery.

'It was then I realised it was financially not viable to go back to work,' Mitchell recalls. 'I would have had to earn a lot to pay for childcare and have anything left.' In London she had a circle of friends with small children, most of whom were keen to get back to the workplace. But with the man earning more in most cases, it ended up being the woman who took on the caregiver role. Others found they had to go back to work part-time. 'They were educated and accustomed to feeling valued at work,' Mitchell says. 'I wanted to be independent and earn my own income, but we longed for another child. I refused to have another baby as long as we stayed in London – I needed more support. It became psychological – what was my worth, what was the point of my going back to work? There was pressure for Phil to earn big bucks. In the end we were convinced we had to move to Sweden if we wanted another child.'

Back in Stockholm, Mitchell called the social services. They asked when Theo was born – and handed the couple 480 days paid time off work, to be used before he reached the age of eight. The authorities made an estimate of what Mitchell would be earning had she been employed, using it to calculate the money she would receive. 'It's so easy, you just fill in your details,' she explains. 'You don't have to do anything, every-thing is taken care of for you.' She found a kindergarten, or *dagis*, near their apartment that would take Theo any time between 8am and 5pm, five days a week – for around £85 a month. 'It was a completely different story from London, such a contrast,' she says. 'I struggled mentally with our first child, because I was so used to taking control of my own life. London and Stockholm were like night and day. If I mention all this to Americans their heads just explode!'

Daughter Freja came along a year after the Mitchells moved to Sweden. There was another difference: no one raised an eyebrow if she or her husband left work early to pick up a sick child. 'What would we do without VAB? It is fabulous,' she says. Or vabulous, perhaps? VAB stands for *vård av barn*, or 'care for the child'. VAB means parents can take up to 120 paid days off work a year to be with a sick child aged up to 12.

Parents, you may have mixed feelings about reading further. The reality many face when they come to give birth in their home countries is likely to be very different from the picture outlined here. Women who have already been through this difficult period in their lives might feel regret: so this is what it could have been like? What if the other parent and I had had these opportunities? How different could our lives have been, and those of our children? Sweden's system of extended parental leave, heavily subsidised nurseries, and generous time off to be with sick children is certainly no panacea. Having a family is hard work, physically and emotionally, and particularly for women. But in terms of support for working parents and families, Sweden is way out in front compared to most of the globe.

Sweden's tax-and-spend approach to raising the next generation opens a fresh, more modern and political perspective on the Swedish model. The country is increasingly identified internationally with the way it champions women's rights; for Swedes themselves who travel or work abroad, the childcare system at home stands out.

When I got together with my future wife Annika in London in 2011, she wanted to go home to have babies. Many Swedish women living abroad feel the call of home most strongly when they think about starting a family. 'They have really dreadful childcare in Switzerland,' says a mother on an internet forum discussing the situation for Swedish women abroad. 'It is shit expensive in Canada, and there is no VAB,' says another. 'No VAB in Spain either,' says a third. 'Due to childcare costs in the UK, and the lack of VAB, it is still very common for one of the parents not to work – mostly the mother,' says a fourth. 'There doesn't appear to be a country that can compare with Swedish parental benefits. It's a jungle out there.'

Hannah Raffelsberger is a New Zealander who has worked all over the world. She fell pregnant with her first child in San Francisco, which turned out to be the beginning of the end of her life in the US. 'It cost $5,000 to give birth in hospital, but I was insured,' she says. 'But the company I worked for wouldn't give me any paid days off after having my child. That was a deal breaker, the end of my working career in the States.' American friends told her stories about having to save up to stay at home with a baby, and day care being 'crazy expensive'. So she quit the job and moved to Austria, where her husband was at medical school. Later the family moved to New Zealand, where Raffelsberger worked full-time. Things were a little easier than the US, but still very tough. Soon she was spending a 'huge chunk' of her salary on day care, or about NZ$500 (£260) a week. 'You start asking yourself: apart from your mental health, what is the benefit of going to work? You are just working to live.'

In New Zealand, Raffelsberger could take just five paid sick days a year, regardless of whether it was for herself or to look after her child. She and husband Jens, who has joint Swedish-Austrian citizenship, moved to Sweden in 2004 when their eldest was three years and their daughter was two months old. 'We were not aware of the rights we had. Social services announced that we were eligible for a retrospective payment – two whole years of child allowance. Jens and I looked at each other and said: "Wow!"' Child allowance was worth about £85 a month. The couple had a third child, and both parents were able to stay home for several months. 'When the children were small they went to day care, it was so nice, they made me feel good about dropping the children off,' she recalls.

The Raffelsbergers then spent some years away from Sweden, returning in 2014 to settle in a small town in the south. This time Hannah appreciated the flexibility for working mothers – she had the right to work part-time if she wanted, varying the hours to suit the family. Her youngest would finish school at 1.30pm, but could have after-school activities until 5 or 6 o'clock. The children could also sign up for low-cost sports programmes. At no cost, her 15-year-old daughter was fitted with braces for her teeth; in New Zealand it would have cost NZ$10,000. 'Swedes are definitely pro family and pro developing the young human being to a fuller extent,' Raffelsberger says. 'The whole mentality is that children who come from less fortunate backgrounds should have the same experiences as others.'

Since the foundations of Sweden's childcare provision were laid in the 1970s, the system has expanded enormously. Childcare has gone from an economic necessity to being a part of Sweden's self-identity.

Chapter 14
Equality

It all began with more rights for men...

In 1974, Sweden became the world's first nation to explicitly allow fathers to take paid time off from work to look after a small child. This reform meant that couples could share six months of parental leave, on 90 per cent of their pay, over the first eight years of the child's life. Mothers already had this right, but sharing it with fathers was a big step in a sustained campaign to usher more women into the workforce by encouraging employment before childbirth, with the right to return to their former workplace after maternity leave. There were few who expected significant numbers of fathers to take up the offer of sharing childcare, but this was still a landmark – for the first time, a national government had acknowledged that parenthood and nursing were not just for women, but also for men.

Putting the case for men to do more childcare, Olof Palme, the enigmatic left-wing aristocrat who led the country at the time, described the outcome of the debate within Swedish society that led to this reform: 'In order that women shall be emancipated from their antiquated role, the men must also be emancipated,' he said. 'The aim over the long run must be that men and women should be given the same rights, obligations and work assignments in society. This fundamental idea is today embraced by almost all political parties in Sweden.' However, as Palme also admitted, this way of thinking was 'still in a strident contrast to the factual conditions'.

Before these changes were set in motion, Swedish women had been largely viewed as inhabiting specific gender roles as housewives and mothers; in the 1950s, Sweden had a lower participation rate of women in the workforce than Britain. However, from the 1960s, Swedish women were encouraged to take jobs to meet Sweden's acute post-war labour shortage. With this evolution came the insight that an altered role for women required changes in the role of men. Slogans about the positive consequences for fathers of sharing domestic tasks were just a start. 'We have to expand society's facilities for childcare,' Palme said. 'When women as well as men go out to work, society has to be organised accordingly. This is vital in order to provide children with a stimulating and diversified environment in which to grow. It fortifies women's ambitions to achieve equality in working life.'

With the die cast, and Swedish politicians and businesses largely in favour of both parents going to work, there was a pressing need to expand provision of childcare outside the home to meet the needs of working couples. Female participation in the economy grew steadily – by the early 1990s women constituted nearly half of the Swedish labour force, the highest percentage anywhere in the world. The blue-collar trade union federation LO became a leading advocate for public childcare, as its women members demanded support. The union's calls complemented the agenda of business and the state to foster an environment in which women could work outside the home while still having children, thereby aiming for full employment alongside relatively high birth rates. The number of publicly provided childcare places increased rapidly, from less than 12,000 in 1965 to over 136,000 by 1980. Simultaneously, the amount of paid time off for parents grew to nine months in 1978, 12 months in 1980 and 15 months in 1989.

Yet men stubbornly refused to take up the chance to spend time with their children. In the scheme's first year men took only 0.5 per cent of all paid parental leave. The centre-right government that kicked out Palme in 1976 launched an advertising campaign featuring weightlifter Lennart Dahlgren, nicknamed 'Hoa-Hoa' for his habit of roaring himself into a frenzy before a lift. With his mane of red hair, Dahlgren was depicted cradling a baby on his bicep in a national poster campaign to encourage men to take paternity leave. It had little or no impact. When the right came to power again in 1991, in the midst of a severe economic slump, the number of fathers taking paternity leave had stalled at 6 per cent.

But this crisis government was not just concerned with the immediate problems of a banking collapse. For Bengt

Westerberg, the Liberal Party leader who was now minister for social affairs in a very pro-business administration, this was an opportunity to tackle a problem that had long concerned him – gender inequality and men's non-existent role in childcare. During the 1980s, Westerberg had railed against the effects of discrimination against women. 'The lack of gender equality is not only an injustice against the women and men who suffer, it also means failing to make use of human resources,' he told parliament. For Westerberg, a middle-aged civil servant whose parents ran the family paint shop south of Stockholm, inequality was about economic inefficiency. 'Gender discrimination and rigid thinking are wasteful. Especially in times of financial difficulties, we need to use each person's individuality, initiative, and willingness to take responsibility. Women have a lot to offer the labour market, business and politics. Men have a lot to offer and are needed for work in the home and with children.'

Westerberg now set out to raise the number of men taking paternity leave. Following intense political debate, the government decided to force men to take at least a month. This 'daddy month' reserved for fathers became law in 1995. Sweden was not the first – Norway had taken a similar step two years earlier. 'I always thought if we made it easier for women to work, families would eventually choose a more equal division of parental leave by themselves,' Westerberg told *The New York Times* some years later. 'But I gradually became convinced that there wasn't all that much choice. … Society is a mirror of the family. The only way to achieve equality in society is to achieve equality in the home.'

The new law had an immediate impact. A Child Care Act obliged city councils to provide care for children aged 12 months and upwards 'without unreasonable delay'. Stockholm also placed a cap on what councils could charge, making the system even more affordable. Subsidised childcare places expanded to nearly 730,000 by 2002. So despite the economic crisis of the early 1990s, Sweden still managed to expand its system of childcare dramatically, at a time when it was cutting back on other aspects of the welfare state.

The young men with a few days' worth of stubble whom you see around town pushing their buggies to the nearest café are known as 'latte dads'. Today, fathers take around a quarter of the total parental leave on average; one in ten couples divide it 40:60 between father and mother, which is twice as many as in the 1990s. In 2002, a second month of compulsory paternity leave was introduced; debate over the measure was muted this time because the principle had already been established. A third compulsory 'daddy month' was added in 2016. Men also use about a third of the available days off for VAB – those paid 120 days per year off to be with a sick child.

Expectations have changed, with more women assuming that their partner will share the childcare, and more companies relaxed about male workers who have kids disappearing for a time. Indeed, some businesses top up employees' incomes when they take parental leave, after earnings compensation was trimmed during the 1990s recession. Sweden spends four times as much of its wealth on early childhood education and care than the United States, or around 1.6 per cent of its GDP. About half of this goes on the cost of paid parental leave. In total, parents pay slightly more than 10 per cent of the gross costs of childcare, with the state and the municipalities covering the lion's share. The law states that families should never pay more than 4 per cent of their income on childcare. The country spends half as much again on 'economic security' for families and children than on defence.

So where does this leave Sweden? For almost half a century the country has been out in front in terms of subsidised childcare and paid time off for parents with small children. It has taken several bold initiatives, each of which has demanded years of debate and preparation. The driving forces have been both economic, as Sweden sought to maximise the potential of its indigenous workforce, and political, as social democratic and liberal politicians pursued an ideal of equality between men and women as a goal in itself. In consequence, the system for enabling women to work and have children looks similar today to how it was in 1974 – just bigger and better.

The private sector was allowed to enter the childcare market a generation ago, but three-quarters of kindergartens are still municipal services, while most of the others are provided by employee and parent cooperatives. Private for-profit childcare has not expanded much beyond the wealthy suburbs of Stockholm, in contrast to elderly care, for example, where services have become less universal and more selective. All childcare facilities are tightly controlled and regulated by councils and the state. So it is in the family sphere that the traditional Swedish welfare state is strongest, still adhering to the values of social equality and fair distribution of life chances that it was born with in the 1970s.

While most rich nations have seen an expansion of family policy in recent decades, Sweden sticks out as a consistent champion of feminism and gender equality, says Kenneth Nelson, professor of comparative social policy at Stockholm University: 'The family is the area that stands out as being pretty much unique – in other areas, Sweden is moving relatively closer to the liberal welfare state as in the UK and US.' Family policy, parental leave and childcare have not suffered from substantial cutbacks, rather they have expanded even further, as these policies are not such a politically contested issue as elsewhere. Even the economists think it's a good thing, not least in terms of increasing the labour force and employment – you make it possible for two-earner households, so it's good for the economy as a whole. 'That's one of the major reasons these policies have been unaffected,' Nelson adds.

There is remarkable political unity over family policy. The small Christian Democrat party has campaigned for more 'choice' for parents to decide how to raise their children, proposing a care allowance that would make it possible for parents of young children to stay at home longer than the time allotted by the parental leave system, or to employ a domestic nanny instead of using public childcare. But low take-up of such a scheme after 2008 meant it was later scrapped. The far-right Sweden Democrats (SD), who are a more significant force in Swedish politics, are hostile to feminism, but even more hostile towards Islam. The party has increasingly used the idea that gender equality is a feature of Swedish culture as a means of focusing on differences and emphasising women's oppression by Islam.

One of the architects of Sweden's recovery from its 1990s economic woes has a point when he identifies family policy as integral to the Swedish model. Göran Persson, the Social Democratic prime minister from 1996 to 2006, says: 'Parental leave is rational. Sweden makes it possible to combine a professional career with the responsibility for two or three kids.' If female university students feel they have to choose between becoming a mother or a professional, many would opt to be professionals, de-prioritising family life. 'A society without children will end up in a very difficult situation. The 66-year-old is not a driving force for economic growth, it is the six-year-old. In a society dominated by six-year-olds you are forced to discuss climate change and so on, because you are future-oriented. Older people look back and ask why did this not happen, whose fault is it, who should I blame? Look at Trump voters in the US.'

For some, this is evidence of a 'new' Swedish model for the country, one that has moved away from an economic focus on relations between trade unions and employers and towards a closer association with feminist values. The approach has solid roots in society, rather than being an expression of identity politics or Sweden's more recent grandstanding on human rights.

Chapter 15
#MeToo

It is one thing for politicians to sloganise about women's equality, but how does it look for businesses trying to cope with the relatively prolonged absence of staff to have children? For Ronnie Leten, the Belgian chairman of Swedish corporation Ericsson we met earlier, the Swedish system came as a shock. He first moved here from Antwerp in 2009 to become the head of tool-maker Atlas Copco. He recalls his surprise when faced with the length of a woman's maternity leave: 'My attitude was: "Oh my God! She should come back after ten or 18 weeks. I can't cope with it, put the child in day care!"'

Over the next seven years he changed his mind. 'Parenthood is a planned absence. You have a six-month early warning once the woman is pregnant, so you can plan it.' Rather than just the need to fill a vacancy, he believes, this can be a valuable opportunity to rotate talent in the company and try out other people in that job. 'People who step in know it is temporary, so you find a market for people who are willing to do that. You find people motivated to do it, and most likely who will bring something new. And after 12 months there are no emotions – they know the guy is coming back.'

Leten was forced to look again at what employees need to stay motivated over the longer term. The ideal from the company point of view is to keep the whole team together, 'working their butts off and having fun,' he says. 'But is that sustainable? You need to have relaxation time, a balance between private life and work.' It was his son with his two small kids who opened Leten's eyes to the pressures faced by families in which both parents work. Now, his attitude to parental leave in Sweden has undergone a transformation. 'I would not even call it generous – they give young couples a very respectful gift from society,' he says. 'This little boy or girl is your responsibility to grow it up in a warm nest and make sure it becomes a fantastic contributor to society. Putting them in day care after ten weeks – is that really the sort of society we want? That's how I see we should interpret it.'

This is another allusion to the long term, and the wider loyalties of businesspeople to society, that we encountered in Part 3. In the same vein, Tom Johnstone, a Scot and a board member of several Swedish corporations, has a neat response to those who doubt the benefits of generous parental leave: 'Obviously it doesn't damage business because otherwise you wouldn't have so many successful businesses here,' he says. 'There is a cost to it – you just have to manage it.' Like Leten, Johnstone takes the broader view: 'The bond formed between parents and baby early on is so important. Here in Sweden we focus much more on wellbeing and equality – and I truly feel we get the benefit in business.'

Hans Enocson, former boss of GE in Sweden, says something similar about women taking long periods of maternity leave: 'I feel the challenge, but it is worthwhile. I believe in a society where you can be a balanced individual. My colleagues in different parts of the world find it very strange: in Germany it is part of the culture for women to stay home, while in the US maternity leave is a few weeks. What counts is productivity, loyalty, having people who enjoy working for the company. And then they pay you back.' Whatever happens to parents is not something employers have to worry about – the systems are in place, all arranged by the government. Sorted.

This is a politically correct point of view, and managers are wary of courting controversy on this issue. 'It is a forbidden topic, you have to behave properly,' says Håkan Mogren of Investor group. 'It is impossible to cut maternity leave because it is taken for granted. I never touch this subject because it is so hot.' However, there is evidence that favourable attitudes among top bosses reflect a more general shift of opinion in economic circles. Philip Hwang, a psychology professor at Gothenburg University, has been surveying companies' attitudes since 1993. In 2009, he and his American colleague Linda Haas reported 'dramatic improvement' in corporate support within large Swedish companies for fathers taking leave, measured in terms of formal policies, informal support from co-workers and managers, and the observation that periods of paternity leave become the norm. The biggest change was the introduction of formal paternity leave policies, which were in place at more than four out of ten companies.

'Swedish parental leave policy,' the researchers concluded, 'appears to have been successful in reducing corporate resistance toward fathers taking leave, helping to make fatherhood more visible at work.' Employers' attitudes were an important factor in fathers taking less time off with kids, as were other dads in the workplace doing so, or working in women-dominated workplaces. The public sector was friendlier towards fathers than the private sector, and there was a class aspect: fathers used more parental allowance if their income was high.

But the researchers also found that family-friendly policies are still regarded as more of a benefit for women than men, because the belief has lingered that being a caregiver is a natural role to which women are better suited. 'The male norm of full-time employment remains strong even in Sweden,' Hwang said in 2016. Fewer than half of mothers go back to work full-time after having a baby, while almost all men work full-time after paternity leave. Generous family support has increased the number of working women, but much of that has been in part-time work; for example, half the women members of the LO trade union federation are part-time.

Meanwhile, women are less likely to be in management and professional occupations. Swedish women experience a large drop in relative earnings following the birth of their first child, and the gap is larger in the top jobs, consistent with the idea of a 'glass ceiling' that limits women from moving up an organisation. Extended absence of someone in a top job is particularly expensive, so companies tend to place relatively few women in fast-track career positions. Some women, who would otherwise be strongly career-oriented, know that their promotion possibilities are limited and may respond by choosing more family-friendly jobs and careers – and by taking more parental leave than their partners. As a result, gender segregation in the economy becomes a self-fulfilling prophecy because of the behaviour of employers and workers alike. So long as family responsibilities are unequally shared, the gender gap is not likely to narrow significantly, even in a highly flexible labour market such as Sweden's.

The global #MeToo movement had a major impact on Sweden in 2017 and 2018, bringing tens of thousands of stories of sexual harassment in the workplace out into the open. Most famously, 18 women made allegations against the husband of a member of the Nobel literature prize committee; he was later jailed for rape. Women at the top of Swedish industry complain about a pattern of informal put-downs, condescension and downright discrimination, despite Sweden's right-on policies and rhetoric. 'In most families, the husband drops the children off in the morning and the mothers pick them up – that's an issue for women in the workforce,' says Karin Forseke, former chief executive of Swedish investment bank Carnegie, when she was one of very few female bosses of companies listed on the Stockholm Stock Exchange. 'Women will leave at 3pm or 4pm to collect the kids, but the fathers can work late and go out for a beer after work,' she says. 'Today it is still women who carry the greatest burden. There are unconscious biases and stereotyp- ical behaviour, this is still a patriarchal society.'

Forseke says she felt more valued when she worked in the United States, where she found success was measured in results, regardless of race or gender. Swedes hide behind the slogans of the Swedish model, Forseke says, preferring to believe that things are 'the best in the world', instead of looking below the surface and outside the country for other ways of doing things. 'We should have a more open and frank discus- sion, but we are very afraid of that,' she says. 'Every system has its strengths and weaknesses, and other parts of the world do certain things better. Parental leave is holy, how can you attack it? But time off should be shared equally between men and women. Otherwise it holds women back.'

Long maternity leave means that women lose time when they could be developing their careers, says Anna Bråkenhielm, a serial entrepreneur who established an organisation called Passion for Business to help women reach the top. She wrote her first newspaper column about the issue in 2002, and since then the number of women in top jobs has changed by only a few per cent. Sweden is too liberal in allowing families to decide who should stay at home with the baby, she argues – parental leave should be divided equally between mother and father. 'If you look at who owns companies and wealth it is men; women are not willing to risk or sacrifice their personal lives and families. If you are a business person and a man you are excused from looking after the home,' Bråkenhielm says. As a man you won't have a bad conscience about being away from your family, she adds, while a woman always has to say sorry. Her mother, a doctor and politician, always complained about the burden of work, but didn't want to admit that deep down she loved her job. Bråkenhielm has made adjustments to her own life: 'I talk to my teenage kids about how much I enjoy my work and travelling, I want them to see me happy in my job. Things are changing in the right direction, but very slowly.'

Bråkenhielm refers to the 2015 scandal that shook Sweden's corporate elite after journalists exposed a culture of lavish perks and extravagance (see Chapter 12). The scandal was widely reported as evidence of a closed and incestuous world in which executives lived by different rules to everyone else. But Bråkenhielm says it was also proof of the overwhelming dominance of men in the corridors of corporate power. 'The scandal shows that it was a male bastion, a closed structure with no women, the same guys all the time.'

One Swedish woman to make it to the top in a very masculine environment is Petra Einarsson, the first female chief executive of high-tech steel-maker Sandvik Materials Technology (SMT), and now boss of BillerudKorsnäs, a maker of sustainable packaging. Starting at SMT as a trainee after leaving university in 1989, she worked her way up to become Sweden's most powerful businesswoman with her appointment as SMT's chief executive in 2013. She sees herself as a role model, but she is acutely aware that just being female in a top job is not enough, and she is frustrated at the slow pace of change. 'If I hadn't been affected by living for 25 years in a totally male-dominated organisation there would be something wrong with me,' she says wryly in SMT's low-ceilinged offices on Kungsbron, central Stockholm. 'I see every day how women are treated differently from men. But if you start to get frustrated and angry, it becomes difficult to change it.'

Instead, her tactic is to stay calm and challenge men's behaviour: 'The thing is not to make the guys look ridiculous. The men who treat women differently to the way they treat men don't do so to be mean or because they are bad people, but because they are accustomed to doing it. If you hold up a mirror to them, they always say: "Really? Oh no, I don't want to be like that." If you challenge a man, they will see their attitudes and behaviour, and so change is possible. Then you have contributed by helping men to see. That is my tactic to cope with it, rather than internalising it and complaining afterwards: "Did you see what happened in that meeting?"'

Getting more women interested in technology means making them feel welcome and talking about what companies like hers can do – that they are not all about machines, and if you come to Sandvik you can make a positive difference. 'We are creating sustainable technologies that will change the world; here you could have more impact on the world than if you become a doctor,' Einarsson says. 'Clean water, safe nuclear plants, lower carbon emissions – they all demand technological shifts.'

As the first female boss in Sandvik's 150-year history, Einarsson feels the under-representation of women at the top of business is a 'failure' for Sweden. The situation for women has improved – men taking time off with children is a huge change from not being home at all. 'So there is hope for the future,' she says. 'But gender diversity is taking too long, it is such a struggle to increase the numbers. Sometimes I think: I am a woman, I am in charge, I should just fix it. But it is not so easy.'

Chapter 16
The People's Home

They were weighing the nappies. Or rather, they were weighing the pee in the nappies. To see how much a resident urinated, staff weighed their soiled incontinence pads. The idea was that they could learn when the elderly person's nappy was likely to be 'full' and needed to be replaced, to minimise the number of 'unnecessary' changes, therefore saving money for the company. 'It is terrible for the elderly, but also for us who have to spend the whole morning weighing pensioners' used diapers,' said a staff member, as employees came forward to blow the whistle on Koppargården retirement home in Stockholm. Worried staff and relatives made a string of allegations. Management tried to silence the relatives of a man who died soon after moving to the home, his daughter said. She found him alone and covered in his own faeces. 'He had been lying and screaming for help but nobody came. He was never himself again after that,' she said.

The scandal at Koppargården, owned by private care company Carema, sparked a national debate about provision of elderly care by for-profit companies. It went to the heart of the unease felt by many Swedes towards an increasing use of the private sector to provide public services funded by the taxpayer. Elderly care was just one aspect of far-reaching changes to Sweden's famed welfare state, and the scandal gives us an alternative perspective on the lenticular image of generous parental leave and family support. Until the 1990s, the country's extensive cradle-to-grave social services were virtually a monopoly, in which the public sector not only funded but also provided the services. Private provision of tax-funded eldercare was almost non-existent in the 1980s, but today it makes up more than a fifth of residential and homecare provision. The Carema affair continues to colour the discussion, not least because its owners included US private equity company KKR, with its reputation for hard-nosed profit-seeking. Opinion polls at the time suggested that the majority of Swedes were opposed to companies making *any* profits at all in the welfare sector, and the question of 'profits from welfare' has remained high on the political agenda ever since.

Sweden's experiment with private-sector involvement in its schools has also come under intense scrutiny. No other European country has entrusted so much of its school system to private companies. In the early 1990s, the government introduced school choice with the aim of boosting performance through competition. It also allowed for the establishment of independent 'free' schools – privately run, for-profit schools that are publicly funded through a voucher scheme. Around one-fifth of children now attend these free schools.

At first, the system was held up as a model for expanding the market in education, winning the admiration of free-market advocates round the world. One such supporter was Michael Gove, the UK's former education secretary, who declared in 2008: 'We need a Swedish education system.' But poor results in the OECD's influential Pisa school performance rankings outraged parents and sparked a national debate on the future of Swedish education. No other country in the survey suffered a steeper decline in reading, mathematics and science results during the first decade of the century – a period when the country's share of top performers in mathematics roughly halved.

At the same time, the education sector has endured scandals of its own. JB Education, owned by Danish private equity, declared itself bankrupt in 2013, causing panic among its 10,000 students. Shortly afterwards, Swedes were appalled by reports that a chain of kindergartens had cut its food budget to around £1 per child per day, and that toddlers were being fed just bread and water (well, crispbread and water – this was Scandinavia after all). The OECD called for sweeping changes. The market in Sweden had failed to learn from the good examples, it said: 'There are some very successful free schools, but the system has not taken advantage of them, while the underperforming ones have not been tackled.'

Wherever you look, in the past three decades there have been major changes to the welfare state, with controversy never far away. In 1998, Sweden became one of the first nations in Europe to scrap defined benefit pensions and replace them with a system in which every Swede invests their retirement money in privately managed funds, the performance of which depends on the ups and downs of stock markets. The self-evident social goal of a pension system – to maintain the living standards of the elderly – now became a secondary concern, critics argued, by making pensioners' incomes dependent on market forces outside their control.

Sweden's healthcare system is superb, but it is not free – each contact with a professional costs money, and drugs are expensive. The number of hospital beds has fallen to the lowest per capita in the developed world, ahead of only Mexico and Chile, while the lengthening queue for operations has fuelled talk of a healthcare crisis. Maternity services have been particularly hard hit, with recent media reports of women giving birth in cars because their local clinic had closed down.

Social policy more generally has been strongly influenced by the New Public Management movement enthusiastically adopted by the UK in the 1980s, aiming to run public-sector bodies more like businesses. This has resulted in an increase in privatisation, competition and consumerism, and of course, budget cuts. When I first moved to Sweden, I had a job at the journalism department at Gothenburg University. In ignorance, I thought I had arrived in the land of milk and honey, a social democratic paradise of well-funded tertiary education. So it came as a shock when I was made redundant a few months later because of big cuts to the department's budget, thanks to a new method for calculating the rent it paid on its premises. My overworked colleagues were dropping like flies after 'hitting the wall', the Swedish equivalent of burnout.

Alongside the market for welfare services have come fat salaries and lavish share options for those at the top of private companies in the sector, some of whom have become easy targets for the media. After Carema changed its name and put controversy behind it, its new boss found himself earning £350,000 a year and owning shares worth nearly £4 million. Welfare millionaires also number the left among them. Former Social Democrat politician and serial welfare entrepreneur Jan Emanuel Johansson made roughly £20 million in 2010 when he sold his business running care homes for troubled young people. When Sweden began receiving a large number of asylum seekers (see Part 6), he started a profitable business taking government money to house and feed them. Entrepreneurs who made a fast buck in this sector included a former right-wing politician who had earlier led a political party that wanted to cut the number of asylum seekers.

Discussions of the welfare state in Sweden inevitably hark back to the 'people's home', or *folkhemmet*, a concept first floated by Social Democrats in 1928, which was solidified after 1945. The people's home became synonymous with the Swedish model of the strong welfare state. 'The basis of a home is community and common sense,' the party's leader Per Albin Hansson famously said, describing a vision of a country without social or economic divisions. 'A good home does not know privileged or underprivileged, favourites or stepchildren. No one looks down on others. No one tries to gain an advantage.... In a good home, equality, care, cooperation and helpfulness prevail.' Many Swedes feel nostalgic for the certainties and stability that they associate with the heyday of the People's Home, when the reality of welfare provision seemed to match Hansson's lofty ambition. Populist politicians today pledge to restore it, offering consensus and community in place of fragmentation and polarisation.

The public sector in Sweden today is a lean – and sometimes mean – welfare machine, in comparison to a generation ago. 'In the Swedish case there have been quite tremendous changes,' says social policy professor Kenneth Nelson. 'I would not say there is no Nordic model any more, but I question the idea whether Sweden belongs to the traditional social democratic welfare state.' Nelson compared unemployment benefits in Sweden with other industrialised nations, and found they were the most generous in the early 1990s, perfectly in line with the old Swedish model. By 2010, however, Sweden was at the other end of the spectrum. Regarding sickness benefits, the level of income replacement is still high, but it is harder to qualify for them, and when you do the period of entitlement is shorter. Sweden's long-term disability provision is now worse than the advanced country average, Nelson says.

The 'people's home' still provides a resilient safety net for most of the people most of the time. Private-sector providers can offer excellent services – who cares what colour the cat is, as long as it catches mice? The debate over Carema's elderly care home at Koppargården was justified, but it took aim at the wrong target, say critics such as Thord Eriksson, a liberal writer and author of a book on elderly care. The key issue is regulating to ensure a high quality of services, not limiting the level of profits, he argues. Care quality at Koppargården was already problematic before it was privatised: 'We talked about profits and we forgot about the rest. It was a shortcut – the general discussion about quality in elderly care is much more complex than just profits.' As for weighing diapers, you can find references to the practice in Swedish healthcare literature long before the Carema scandal, as a method for choosing the appropriate incontinence product. Linking the practice to profit-seeking was perhaps a cheap shot at the private sector.

In the context of the new people's home, with its emphasis on efficiency and performance, the generosity of Sweden's family policies stands out in even sharper contrast. In other areas of the welfare state, the country has embarked on large-scale experiments in allowing the market to deliver public services. The jury is still out, and the future direction unclear.

PART 6

IMMIGRATION

Chapter 17
Riot

A smell of burning tyres mingled with the scent of cherry blossom that grew so thick it seemed every tree was detonating in a soft, pink explosion. This was May 2013, and I had just set foot in Stockholm. The short nights of early summer meant there were still several hours of daylight ahead when I dropped my bags and walked up the hill into Husby. This small suburb was making international headlines because its youth was in revolt, torching cars and fighting with the police. When I got the call, I was sitting in a dull conference on corporate governance in a village on the west coast. It was all kicking off in Stockholm, but the *Financial Times* correspondent for the region had just boarded the slow boat to Legoland in Denmark with his son. This made me nearest to the story. I didn't need to be asked twice to get myself to the capital.

It seemed like an unlikely place for a riot. The walkways between the apartment blocks were quiet, lined with well-kempt verge and rhododendrons. At the top of the hill I entered a setting I would see again and again in Swedish suburbs after I immigrated permanently a few months later – a narrow, drab pedestrian area, lined by a few single-storey shops clad in grey concrete. But tonight it was full of people. Black and brown people. Mainly men, of all ages, some dressed in the flowing tunics and baggy trousers of their original homelands. Nobody paid me the slightest attention – there were serious things afoot. I adopted a tactic that has since stood me in good stead, proffering a big smile and asking: 'Do you speak English?' For two days and nights I tramped around Husby, talking to anyone and everyone, notebook in hand. A Tunisian called Abdul took me under his wing and helped me to eavesdrop on conversations.

The crowds I met on that first night were not rioting – they were out to try and stop the rioters, remonstrating with the young men who were throwing stones, burning cars and trashing schools. For that brief week in May, the cup of discontent ran over among Sweden's immigrant youth. A sense of injustice had been building for years. Husby felt like a ghetto, with sub-standard housing and people trapped on welfare, unable to get jobs. Facilities for young people had closed down, schools were overcrowded and underfunded. This is the story of immigrant Sweden. Every large town has one or more areas like this, where you cross the road and suddenly every face is dark-skinned. Today the share of the population with a foreign background in Husby is more than 70 per cent, predominantly from Africa and the Arab world. In neighbouring Rinkeby, which became notorious a few years later for shootings and gang violence, it is 90 per cent.

The rioters were second-generation youth, born in Sweden, speaking Swedish and feeling themselves to be Swedes. All repeated the same story – they were treated as second-class citizens by white Swedish society. Yunis, from Yemen, had kept his teenage son at home that week. He had high hopes for his star pupil, but feared that attitudes would make it hard for him to get work. 'Maybe I should change his name,' Yunis said. 'They see Ali or Abdul or whatever, and that's it, suddenly there is no job.'

The intensity of the 2013 unrest shocked the world. France and Britain had experienced riots in recent years, but Sweden was supposed to be different. How could a high-wage, high-welfare society coexist alongside pockets of deprivation? How could the country's leaders claim to represent a 'humanitarian superpower' – spending proportionately more of the nation's income on foreign aid than most other countries – at the same time as they presided over extreme levels of segregation and inequality at home?

Furthermore, this was the year in which the great refugee exodus to Europe from the war-torn Middle East and Africa was gathering momentum. At its peak two years later, Sweden received 163,000 asylum seekers, the highest number per capita after Hungary, which took far fewer than Sweden in the preceding and following years. In the five years to 2016 – after which numbers dropped sharply – Sweden received 370,000 asylum seekers, or 3.5 per cent of its total population. According to the official figures, more than half of these – including relatives who came to join them – were granted temporary or indefinite permission to remain. Could the model find them jobs, somewhere to live, schools for their children and help them become productive contributors to society?

At first, political leaders expressed a soaring humanitarianism that seemed to border on the naive. Prime Minister Fredrik Reinfeldt, leader of Sweden's conservative centre-right, urged Swedes to 'open their hearts' to refugees; the speech may have cost him his job. Many felt he was asking them to 'open their wallets', with taxpayers subsidising the liberal elite's multiculturalist fantasies. Having lost the 2014 election, Reinfeldt defended himself: 'I often fly across the Swedish countryside and I would advise more people to do that,' he said. 'There are endless fields and forests. There is more space than you can imagine. Those who claim that the country is full, they should show us where it is full.' Was the former prime minister really suggesting that Sweden's size alone meant it could cope with unlimited immigration at a whirlwind pace? It presented the anti-immigrant Sweden Democrats party with an open goal. New arrivals needed infrastructure, housing, schools and healthcare, they said.

A year later, in 2015, a thousand asylum seekers were crossing into the country every day from Denmark, drawn by tales of Swedish generosity and understanding. Turning out to welcome them, the centre-left Prime Minister Stefan Löfven told a crowd of Stockholmers that his vision of Europe was one that receives people fleeing from war: 'My Europe does not build walls, we help when the need is great.' What seemed like a tough job would, in the long run, be an asset for Sweden, he said. This attitude, an embodiment of Reinfeldt's 'open your hearts', lasted about two months, to be replaced by nothing short of panic. In November, the government slammed the door shut and imposed tough measures to deter asylum seekers. 'It pains me that Sweden is no longer capable of receiving asylum seekers at the high level we do today. We simply cannot do it any more,' Löfven announced. His deputy burst into tears. 'The last bastion of humanitarianism has fallen,' a United Nations official told me. Refugee arrivals in Sweden plummeted overnight.

But now refugees were here, what was Sweden going to do? On the European and North American right, a narrative emerged – large-scale immigration was a disaster and Sweden would be punished for its generosity with rising crime and violence. The country was set up as a whipping boy for multiculturalism, a deterrent to any moves to allow more migrants into Europe and the United States. This account went viral in February 2017, when the newly elected US president, Donald Trump, claimed that a terror attack had taken place 'last night in Sweden', when the night in question had in fact been entirely peaceful. Now the anti-immigrant right set out to prove that Trump was on to something after all, and that Sweden was a country overrun by dark-skinned criminals, rapists, murderers and terrorists. Social media was inundated by allegations of this nature, a prophecy that seemed fulfilled in April when Rakhmat Akilov, a 39-year-old asylum seeker from Uzbekistan, drove a truck into pedestrians on Stockholm's main shopping street, killing five in the name of Islamic State.

Sweden's immigrant areas were now 'no-go zones', the right claimed – a distortion that has become a meme. In a spiral of rhetoric, Swedish officials began referring to 'war zones'; there was even talk of sending in the army.

I have wandered around many of these 'no-go areas' during my time in Sweden, meeting some remarkable people in the process and never experiencing any trouble. I went back to Husby in January 2018. 'We too can dream big' claimed a freshly painted slogan outside the small community centre. But several shops had closed down, including a supermarket, shuttered for more than a year. Young people were smoking cannabis in the stairwells. The library was closed that day because of staff shortages, disappointing a string of young mothers with small children. A new block of flats had just been completed, but the corrugated cladding on the other blocks was stained and shabby. Young black people were notably more suspicious of me than five years previously. 'What's your agenda?' they asked, and complained that nothing had changed. The hairdresser, an Iranian woman, was struggling to keep her business afloat; the politicians were to blame, she said. But at least Husby had calmed down, there was no more rioting or arson. Abdullah, an asylum seeker from Iraq, pointed above his head to a ball of mirror glass – security cameras had been installed everywhere, he said; any trouble and the police were here in minutes. It was hard to find somewhere to live because the black market in apartments had doubled the rents. And learning Swedish here was impossible, because everyone spoke Arabic.

The Husby revolt of 2013, which had been my fiery baptism into Scandinavian life, shone a spotlight on a challenge to the Swedish model that was about to become a prominent question in local and European politics. My conversations with dark-skinned strangers on those long May evenings were an introduction to the country, and also the beginning of an extended period in which I followed the asylum issue for various newspapers at the start of my new life as an immigrant myself – albeit a white, middle-class English one. In interviews for this book with the country's movers and shakers during 2017–18, immigration was a recurring theme; there was a sense that something must be done, urgently, although nobody was really sure what.

'There is a tremendous amount of pushback over the refugees right now – the government and the media are the only people in Sweden who think it's hunky dory,' Stu Graham, the former chief executive of construction group Skanska, remarked. Johan Forssell at the Wallenbergs' Investor group lamented Sweden's 'insider/outsider problem' – people inside the system were happy, but outsiders couldn't find a way in. Sweden is 'not good right now' at integrating immigrants, he said, 'we need to improve'. Seen in historical perspective, 200 years of peace meant Swedes took a lot for granted, creating a short-sighted approach that if something bad happens, 'someone will come to help us,' said Carl Bennet, the biotech billionaire. 'So we discuss problems in a naive way.... The thinking was good on refugees in 2015, but you must plan these things, you must do it in such a way that you can develop it. We shipped water up to our necks. We couldn't handle it.'

Recent immigration policy 'was a mistake', according to Göran Persson, the former centre-left prime minister. 'The big group of immigrants that have arrived in the past ten years – there we have a problem. We are not going to destroy the Swedish model for their sake.' Others said finding jobs and homes for tens of thousands of new arrivals meant the model must change. 'It was such a huge number of people in relation to our population in such a short period that came into the country, it is causing real challenges and real issues,' investment banker Karin Forseke said. 'We are going to have to figure out a way to quickly get them into jobs. We will have to go away from the model if we are to manage this. If we don't manage this well, then we will have serious problems ahead of us. We are seeing it now in the violence and in the whole areas where people are not working, not being integrated. This means having to accept alternatives to our traditional model of high-quality, high-pay jobs. Our system is being tested. We have to wake up to it.'

In the 1980s and '90s the country managed relatively large flows of refugees from Yugoslavia and Iraq. Can it do so again?

Chapter 18
Jobs

Ahmad Saadeha challenges all the stereotypes of a refugee. Just two years after fleeing the war in Syria, the 28-year-old is holding down a job in the IT department at the headquarters of Volvo Group, the global truck-manufacturer based in Gothenburg. With his neatly trimmed beard, fashionable spectacles and good shoes, it is hard to believe that he twice crossed the Mediterranean in a rubber dinghy (the first time, it sank) and made it to Sweden on forged documents. 'I decided I had to take some risks in my life, to think about my children and grandchildren – I didn't want them to experience the same things I did,' he says. After he arrived in Sweden in 2015, he waited 15 months for a decision on his asylum application, sharing a room with other refugees in a small village.

Out of the blue he got an email from Stockholm's Royal Engineering Academy, who had seen his LinkedIn profile. The academy had a programme to help skilled refugees, and they encouraged Saadeha to apply – he had a degree in business administration from Damascus University, he spoke good English and he had experience working for some big companies in Qatar. After numerous applications, he was accepted by Volvo on a four-month internship. Saadeha describes the feeling: 'It was a moment of surrendering to wonder. You cannot imagine what it is like to be a person with nothing, and to get an opportunity.' It meant getting up at 4.30am every morning to be at work by 8am. His internship was extended and turned into a temporary job and then a permanent one. It was perfect: 'I am an active person, a producing, valid person. It has been hectic but it feels so good to have this opportunity. Swedish society has allowed me to do this. I have a commitment to pay back this favour to the community.'

Saadeha was recruited as part of a national programme involving 150 employers and providing around 1,000 internships a year, financed by the government and the Wallenberg family. The aim was to fast-track refugees and other skilled immigrants into work, but there were also benefits for the companies themselves. With the economy growing, and 1.6 million Swedes due to retire by 2025, Sweden would soon be short of tens of thousands of skilled workers, according to Kristian Andersson, Talent Director for Volvo. Moreover, the company was expanding rapidly and needed to employ at least 1,000 workers over the next two years in Sweden alone. 'The competitiveness is intense, there is a war for talent. Therefore we see people coming in as extremely helpful to us, they are resources that we need to stay competitive and to stay successful,' he told me. 'We need to embrace the people coming in.'

The internship programme was an opportunity to test people out. Andersson had other justifications for Volvo's attempts to actively recruit refugees:

> Companies with a diverse workforce perform better, they get more innovative thoughts and products, so they serve customers better. And foreigners open doors for us in markets where we are not so strong, help us understand those markets better. Without diversity you can only develop to a certain extent. If you grow up in the same house, that's your world – with diversity you see the world. We have a global presence and we need to reflect it. Only 2 per cent of our sales are in this country, we are active in 192 markets. By bringing in newcomers to Sweden it enriches you, you see a broader perspective, it turns a local company into a global company.

The easiest approach was still to recruit Swedes, Andersson acknowledged – you know the context, the business doesn't need to adjust as much to include them. But he cited studies suggesting that when you have to work a little to explain things, employees get smarter, they are inspired to try new approaches. And it gives them a more objective platform for making decisions: 'When you are in a Swedish context it will be a Swedish decision,' he said. 'The task I have is to sell the internship programme, to give people good arguments why this is a good idea. But we have so many engaged people who are willing to try, willing to take a stand for what we think is good as a company, and who also see the benefits.' Although the company had recruited only a few dozen white-collar workers this way, in 2018 it was due to expand the programme to blue-collar jobs, mixing internships with training and language lessons.

Here was the Swedish model working well – fast-growing companies focused on world markets, seeing the potential for their businesses of helping refugees into work on the same high wages as everyone else. But would this be enough? In 2016, a large chunk of Swedish business said 'No'. Only half the recent refugee intake had even secondary education – so what about the other half? Just 5 per cent of jobs in the Swedish economy demanded 'no need for special skills', the lowest proportion of all EU countries. Sweden's model of high-skilled, high-wage jobs just couldn't absorb the unskilled refugees, the argument went. Minimum wages in Sweden were twice as high as in most developed countries, making it economically unfeasible to create low-skilled jobs suitable for new arrivals.

You didn't need to be Einstein to see the scale of the mismatch between the productivity levels currently demanded by Sweden's economy, and what most refugees had to offer, said Johan Javeus, chief strategist at Swedish bank SEB. 'In the past, we have spent a lot of resources on educating the workforce to have high-skilled jobs – this is very difficult to do with the high number of refugees,' he said. 'It is a shock to the system, and it is hard to see how the old model will not crumble.' Sweden was nearing a situation where more than half the total unemployed would consist of people born outside the country. Employment rates among low-skilled immigrants were far lower than those of native Swedes, and the lowest among developed countries – it took seven years or more on average for a new arrival to get work. Joblessness among immigrants was also creating a shadow economy with low-paid jobs. The Confederation of Swedish Business claimed that 200,000 new jobs could be generated if salaries were frozen or allowed to fall.

In response, Sweden's centre-left rallied behind a defence of the Swedish model. 'Sweden is at a crossroads. Therefore the Swedish model needs to be strengthened more than ever,' the prime minister declared in early 2016. Introducing 'poverty wages' would deliver a 'major blow' to Swedish competitiveness, the Labour minister added. 'It is an un-Swedish model with inspiration from southern Europe,' where the economies of Spain, Italy and Portugal were based on a far higher proportion of low-skilled jobs, she argued. The trade unions were even more vociferous, accusing the business lobby of 'resorting to apartheid' to lower salaries, using 'a battering ram to attack workers' rights' and placing a 'grenade under the Swedish model'. Instead of giving them low-paid jobs, Sweden would have to educate these people, offer them vocational training and move them up the skills ladder.

Proposals for lower minimum wages were nothing particularly new, however – lower starting salaries had previously been suggested as a solution to unemployment among women and young people, according to Patrik Vulkan, a labour market researcher at Gothenburg University. 'Comparisons between Sweden and the United States, where minimum wages are lower and employment rates far higher among recent immi-grants, are misleading,' he says, 'because Sweden has far more refugees, whereas US immigrants are primarily seeking work. Economic migrants are much more likely to have thought about choosing a destination where their skills are needed, rather than just hoping for the best.'

Nine out of ten refugees in the latest wave were aged under 40, so most had a reasonably full working life ahead of them and would repay the investment they required in educa-tion and skills, the unions maintained. 'The bumblebee shouldn't fly, but it flies really well,' Karl-Petter Thorwaldsson, head of LO, told me in the spring of 2017. 'So we have agreed with the employers to negotiate a new agreement on how to get more refugees into work – the typical Swedish way of solving problems is the pragmatic way.' It took months to a hammer out a deal, which employers and unions then took to the government. They proposed that businesses should pay as little as 8,400 kronor (£685) a month to hire refugees for up to two years, with the state topping up their pay to the national minimum level in each sector. Private sector agencies would match vacancies to refugees, who would, like apprentices, be allowed paid time off to study Swedish and improve their skills.

Could this idea of subsidised apprenticeships succeed, creating entry-level jobs while maintaining high-level wages for everyone else? Patrick Joyce is well qualified to judge – he was a senior adviser on labour markets and integration for Sweden's centre-right government from 2006 to 2014, and a co-author of New Start, a successful subsidised jobs programme designed to help the long-term unemployed. The preconditions for absorbing the new influx of refugees were encouraging, Joyce says: 'So far it looks good – we have economic growth, high employment and labour shortages. But these agreements have failed before.' The centre-right had tried a similar apprenticeship scheme to help young people and immigrants, aiming for 30,000 subsidised places; they managed only 700. 'The unions and the employers didn't really want it. There was an agreement with the government, but when push came to shove they didn't create these jobs,' Joyce says. Also, subsidising work can have unintended consequences. A large share of the taxi drivers in Sweden are immigrants, for example. This is because the taxi companies discovered they could hire most of their drivers through New Start, getting a hefty subsidy from the state. As a result, native Swedes find it harder to become a taxi driver.

Over the long term, Sweden is no better or worse than Germany, the Netherlands or other Nordic countries at getting refugees into work, Joyce says. But it is slow at the beginning, with a much higher proportion out of work during their first years in the country. So would the refugee influx force a shake-up in Sweden's unusual labour market? 'It's unlikely,' he says.

Compromise is messy, but it is the Swedish way.

Chapter 19
Homes

The housing market does not work. Our employees cannot find anywhere to live.

Fix it, or we will quit Sweden.

This was the blunt message to the government from the founders of Spotify, Daniel Ek and Martin Lorentzon, in the spring of 2016. They were trying to recruit young talent to Sweden from all over the world, but the acute shortage of rental accommodation meant moving to Stockholm was unattractive. 'Compare it with cities like New York, London and Singapore where the opportunity to rent housing is very simple,' Ek and Lorentzon wrote. 'We are therefore forced to note that if no changes occur, we need to consider expanding more into other countries instead of Sweden.'

A few months later, Sweden's Housing Board issued a bombshell estimate of how many new homes the country would need if demand was to be met: 700,000 new homes by

2025. This would mean a rate of construction not seen since the 1970s – 'totally different' to the pace of house-building over the past two decades. Adding to the urgency was unexpectedly high immigration.

The housing crisis in Sweden had been growing for years, but the surge of new arrivals moved it up the agenda. For young Swedes, the idea of securely renting or owning their own home had become a disappearing fantasy. According to the Tenants Union, in 2017 almost a quarter of young people in their twenties were still living with their parents, while a similar number were subletting or renting a room. More than half Stockholm's population – nearly 600,000 people – were registered in the queue for a coveted rental apartment, because the tightly regulated rental market meant that rents were relatively low. Getting to the front of the line in central Stockholm took 20 years, while in suburbs like Husby the waiting time in 2016 was more than a decade. Some who lived in overcrowded accommodation were able to jump the queue, but there was no system of prioritising key workers or people in desperate need of a roof over their heads. Rents in new-build apartments were significantly higher because construction companies had been exempted from rent controls; low rents often meant properties required renovation and repair.

The result was a thriving rental property black market, with large bribes changing hands to obtain a home. Many tenants exploited the situation by subletting space – when someone advertised a tiny closet in their apartment, there were many applicants. 'It is almost impossible for immigrants and new arrivals to penetrate this market – it is all about who you know and how much money you have,' said Billy McCormac, head of the Fastighetsägarna property association. Refugees alone would need nearly 40,000 new homes per year in 2015 and 2016, the Housing Board said. Meanwhile, the high demand for homes coincided with cheap loans to produce a house-price bubble – property prices had risen sixfold in 20 years, with homeowners taking on colossal levels of debt. The ratio of household debt to disposable income soared to become one of the highest in the world. The market expanded when large numbers of tenants were given the right to buy – which in turn increased the shortage of rental properties.

A few months after the Spotify letter, the centre-left government announced a 'historic' investment in more housing. The state would make it easier for construction companies to get building permits and planning permission; it would make more land available, and offer billions in subsidies for companies to build low-rent properties in areas where it might not otherwise be profitable to do so. Since 2012, house-building in Sweden had been rising steadily, and it continued to do so after the government announced its package of measures. So it's hard to know whether the relatively high number of new homes built in 2017 was connected to government policy. There were warning signs that the higher pace of house-building might not be sustainable – the forecast for 2018 was for a dip in construction, owing to capacity constraints in the sector. The government's targets were testing builders to the limit. 'Let me put it this way: it is twice the speed of what we are doing today,' said the boss of one of Sweden's biggest construction companies. With politicians promising a quarter of a million new homes in just five years, comparisons were made with the 1960s. There was talk of a new 'Million Programme', echoing the period from 1965 when, to international acclaim, a million new homes were built in just ten years.

Hopes for a new Million Programme are misplaced, says Erik Stenberg, associate professor of architecture at the Royal Institute of Technology, adding that the housing programme, which turned Sweden from having the worst housing stock in Europe to among the best, was the result of careful planning and collaboration over decades – in contrast to today. The first commission to examine the problem was appointed in 1933, and data collection and analysis continued after the war. 'There was a coupling between politics and industry based in the Saltsjöbaden agreement [see Chapter 2], which in turn led to a coupling of quality and quantity – so that we built better as we built more,' Stenberg says. To do that, Sweden had to reorganise the whole of society to produce better housing, which in turn would help to change society: children would have their own rooms, and so get better education, better jobs, then pay more taxes and thereby contribute to the welfare state. Studies were undertaken of how much storage space a typical family would need, and how companies could produce goods to fit into those spaces. IKEA is the prime example of a company that built itself on this standardisation. 'Lots of flexibility was built into the housing to allow for social change,' Stenberg adds. 'Production was driven by the idea of "good living" – if we produce good housing we will get better citizens.'

But this building explosion was brought to an end by the global economic crisis brought on by the 1973 oil price shock, and a sudden shift in Swedish society away from the modernist visions of the 1960s. Although high-rise apartment blocks made up only one-third of the output of the Million Programme, they came to symbolise everything that was considered wrong with it: uniform, standardised, even 'inhuman', Stenberg says. This post-modernist backlash, together with the economic crisis, led to a dramatic collapse in house-building. Construction companies went bankrupt, key people left the industry or retired, and expertise built up over decades was lost. Even archives were destroyed – the reputation of the Million Programme was so bad that nobody wanted anything to do with it.

As a result, 45 years later there is little structural understanding of how to produce a lot of high-quality, affordable homes in a hurry without storing up problems for the future. The early Swedish model gave rise to an approach to house-building that has long been abandoned. Leaving construction to the market, albeit with blandishments from the state, is an experiment that may work, or that may end in a new crisis, Stenberg believes. Indeed, there is also the danger of repeating the other outcome of the Million Programme – producing a lot of new housing that society then turns against. It is precisely the programme's apartment blocks of the 1960s and '70s that are now home to Sweden's recent immigrants. So there is justified scepticism that volume alone can overcome the sharp segregation between white and black areas, and the tendency for the latter to become pools of discontent.

While more homes and cheaper rents are essential, another set of problems needs to be addressed, says Boel Godner, the Social Democratic mayor of Södertälje, a city close to Stockholm where more than half the residents were either born abroad or both parents were. In parts of the district this rises to 85 per cent; in one school just two of its 750 pupils are classified as ethnic Swedish. Famously, since the 2003 invasion of Iraq, the city has accepted more Iraqi refugees than the US and Canada put together. Södertälje became notorious for gang violence in the first decade of this century, but Godner has overseen a successful combination of tough policing and targeted social interventions, and the city now makes headlines again, but for the right reasons.

'The huge migration in 2015 was a wakeup call for the Swedish model – it was like they woke up and found out that it was happening, that so many people were coming from other countries,' Godner says. 'Suddenly the issues that we were talking about for so long are being taken seriously.' For years Godner has insisted that the law enabling refugees to settle anywhere they please should be scrapped, obliging the whole of Sweden to become more ethnically mixed. Planning for each region to take a quota of immigrants – and create sufficient housing to accommodate them – would also increase the chances that refugees would learn Swedish and learn to be Swedes, rather than disappearing into high-density immigrant areas where they are more likely to become cut off from the surrounding society, she believes. 'If refugees had come to every city it would have been different. At present, so many people end up in segregated areas and have problems learning Swedish, yet that is the key to getting a job. This is why it has to be changed.' Every child should go to a school where other children speak Swedish, Godner argues. 'If you find yourself outside, not belonging to society, it is easier to end up unemployed, or used by organised criminals. That has to be changed.'

Building more homes is therefore only part of the solution, she says. It makes no sense for areas such as Södertälje to keep on welcoming large numbers of immigrants while there are so many parts of Stockholm that remain whites-only areas. The black market in housing has to be smashed, with stiff penalties for people who make money by cramming immigrants into small apartments. 'People from other countries should live in every city, that is what makes countries strong and not polarised,' she says. 'Your chance of making it will be so much better if you spend time in a small town with few immigrants while you learn Swedish. Then you can move in an organised way to get a job, an apartment and so on. It may sound hard, but it is the only solution for immigrants to get a good future.'

Chapter 20
Souls on Fire

They organise coffee mornings, jumble sales, children's events, football matches, day trips, legal advice, music evenings, picnics, dances, language classes – anything that brings local Swedes together with the asylum seekers in their midst. Known as *eldsjälar* – 'souls on fire' – groups like this were initially praised by politicians as the way forward for the whole country. Now they are largely ignored, even sneered at. But under the surface they carry on their painstaking work of integrating the new arrivals marooned in communities all over this enormous country. The government provides asylum seekers with a roof over their heads, a bed and three meals a day. And there, more or less, its responsibility ends. Volunteers have stepped in to try to fill the gaps. Sweden also has an official system of guardians who help young asylum seekers settle in. At the last count, there were over 150,000 of these *gode män* – literally, 'good people'.

Civil society has also mobilised to express concerns about asylum seekers. In January 2016, a young female social worker was stabbed to death by a Somali youth in a home for juvenile asylum seekers in Mölndal, a satellite of Gothenburg. The boy was placed in psychiatric care. But the killing led to an outpouring of fears about crime and sexual harassment. Across the city, public meetings were packed with hundreds of sceptical and angry people, anxious that asylum centres would be sited in their neighbourhoods. With the city experiencing an acute housing shortage, there was also exasperation that refugees were getting any accommodation at all.

This is a live debate within Swedish society. Before 2015, immigration was not widely discussed in public, reflecting an establishment consensus that also treated the anti-immigration Sweden Democrats as political pariahs. To an outsider such as myself, it seemed the debate then boomeranged in the opposite direction, with extreme sensitivity in the media to any issues connected to immigration and asylum. While this was surely better than sweeping problems under the carpet, there was still a tendency to see things in black and white – opponents of immigration seized on every problem as proof of impending disaster, while supporters dismissed these reports as a racist conspiracy. The situation was not helped by an absence of official statistics on ethnicity and crime, helping to stoke visceral fears that recent immigration was leading to a rise in rape and violence.

There are forces abroad that want Sweden to fail. After the stabbing tragedy in Mölndal, Britain's popular *Daily Mail* newspaper sent a journalist to the town. His report was titled 'The city destroyed by migration: Inside the Swedish town where armed gangs patrol the streets, crime has exploded and a beautiful social worker's murder has shocked Europe.' The article claimed that Mölndal was facing a 'rising migrant crime wave', its streets 'at the mercy of gangs of young men.' It even talked about 'mass shootings with lots of people killed.' It was illustrated with photographs all taken at night, depicting scenes of apparent social desolation.

This was my home town, and it was a picture I did not recognise. My in-laws had lived here for 40 years, my wife grew up here. So I spoke to many of the people named in the Mail's article. I found people struggling to cope with a difficult situation and stretched resources, but not the picture of social catastrophe depicted by the newspaper. The dark scenes photographed in fact told a story of regeneration – the centre of Mölndal was being totally rebuilt, with bright new office blocks and a gleaming, upmarket shopping mall. Attractive new homes now looked down on the town centre from the hills above. When I met young refugees in the town, I found quiet, sensitive teenagers exploring the potential of their new world. One Somali was training to become a carer for Sweden's elderly, working at McDonald's to pay for his education. He missed his mother painfully. Another had decorated his bedroom walls with pink butterflies.

As for the 'mass shootings', there was a spate of deadly, gang-related violence in a distant part of Gothenburg in 2014–15, but within a year the police had jailed the ringleaders and largely put a lid on it. Sweden has an urgent problem with violent gang crime, but this is a symptom of issues that have been festering for years in poverty-stricken ghettos where hope is in shorter supply than the drugs that fund the gangs.

It would have been a miracle if the large influx of destitute, traumatised people from the world's war zones had not caused tensions. In 2018 it still took more than 500 days to get a decision on an asylum application, during which people were crammed into empty buildings wherever they could be found, not allowed to earn money and unable to speak the language of the country. The fact that there has not been more trouble is testimony to the goodwill of most new arrivals and the people around them. Things are not easy. Across the country, individuals are making choices about how they want Sweden to be, and what they want it to become.

Can the country afford it? Those who welcome refugees often argue that they will benefit Sweden by getting jobs and paying taxes. Opponents say the welfare system will go broke. Both sides are wrong, according to Joakim Ruist, an economist at Gothenburg University and one of the few researchers who has looked at this issue seriously. He estimates on average that each refugee that Sweden takes will cost society £170,000 over the refugee's lifetime. This is not a particularly large sum, but nor is it a positive financial benefit for the country. The uncertainties in the calculation are significant, but Ruist believes that his work has at least prevented politicians from making simplistic claims one way or the other. From 2015 to 2017, the government cut its borrowing and debt fell by about 3 per cent of national economic output, Ruist points out – so the refugee wave did not prevent the government from improving its finances.

At the same time, trust in Sweden's institutions appears to be rising. Each year the respected SOM Institute at Gothenburg University asks Swedes how much trust they have in the way institutions conduct their work. The April 2018 survey showed rising trust in the police, the courts, schools, healthcare and even politicians. Commenting on the results, Andreas Johansson Heinö, deputy head of the liberal think-tank Timbro, wrote: 'Migration policy can be evaluated in different ways, but it has not caused a systemic collapse, at least not in the eyes of the voters. Voters prioritise schools and health, but at the same time they have relatively high confidence in how welfare works. ... In comparison with the political parties, the average voter seems to have plenty of ice in his stomach and been strikingly stable in his attitudes.'

Many of those who argue for tight limits on immigration say that the modern welfare state is likely to be undermined by ethnic diversity because people will start to question the redistribution of wealth to other groups. The jury is out on whether Sweden provides any proof of this hypothesis. Meanwhile, the country's welfare sector needs to hire more than 500,000 new staff over ten years from 2018, according to the annual recruitment estimates by the municipalities and county councils, owing to a rising population of children and the elderly combined with the impending retirement of existing personnel. Those workers need to come from somewhere.

In 1938, the renowned Swedish economist and social scientist Gunnar Myrdal was invited to the US by the Carnegie Corporation to conduct an independent study into 'the Negro problem'. After travelling the country for five years, Myrdal's report, *An American Dilemma*, detailed the situation of black Americans. His conclusions seem appropriate to Sweden's debate over immigration today – and indeed to the US after the rise of Donald Trump:

> It is in this situation of fear, bewilderment, and insecurity that internal disunity can arise. Instead of blaming the real causes, the white majority may put the blame for their difficulties on groups from whom they have traditionally been separated. This is all the easier if there are leaders who, for their own selfish reasons, encourage such splits. Such leaders can rise easily in a democracy and only an alert and interested citizenry can choose between these and honest leaders. Much of European history shows us the internal quarrelling, lack of progress, and general weakness that can result from having a sizeable minority not integrated into the nation or not treated as equals.

PART 7

THE MIDDLE WAY

Chapter 21
Empire

Jacob Wallenberg did not want to be interviewed. Sweden's best-known capitalist oozed boredom, even disdain. One by one he dismissed my list of pre-prepared interview questions, concluding: 'To me these are very shallow. And these are the questions you ask? They seem a bit…' – he paused for emphasis – '…off.'

We were on the 5th floor of Arsenalsgatan 8c, the address near Stockholm's central waterfront from which the Wallenberg family has directed its £200 billion empire for 40 years. It was a grey June morning. A mist of fine rain outside the window added to the gloom inside the office. Interviews with a Wallenberg are like hens' teeth. The family motto, 'to be, not be seen', is apt – it does its best to stay out of the public eye.

Nor did Wallenberg want to be photographed. His adviser explained that Jacob doesn't like to be associated with power, so would rather his photo was not taken here – the place reeks of 'old money'. But Wallenberg had chosen this venue himself. If old money was going to talk, it would do so on its home territory. And wearing a good suit. So instead of suggesting we reconvene at the nearest McDonald's, I decided just to suck it up and let the oracle speak.

The next three chapters consist of interviews with three men who have each, for significant periods of time, had a hand on the tiller when it came to steering Sweden into the 21st century. There is the voice of big business – Jacob Wallenberg's – then one from the left of Swedish politics, and one from the right. As befits people at this level of society, all three men talk with fluency and authority about politics and economics. They have a helicopter view of Sweden, seeing the big picture rather than one or two pieces of the jigsaw. And they weigh every word, anticipating questions and objections – they each have a sense of what is possible in the real world and what is not. While in power they have tested their ideas against reality, helping to take the ideological edge off their views of the world. Each occupied positions where they could be part of taking decisions that actually made a difference. This is what makes them interesting, and important, in terms of understanding how Sweden ticks.

* * *

So – back to the grumpy capitalist. How did the Wallenberg family build a huge and highly profitable business operation while working under governments that appeared far to the left of anything else in Western Europe? How could the left allow one single family to control companies worth 40 per cent of the total value of Stockholm's stock exchange?

Part of the answer seems to be an accident of biology. The eldest son of the founder of the business was a highly successful entrepreneur, but he and his wife had no children. In 1917, they decided to donate their money to a non-profit foundation. This became the basis of the Wallenberg approach: family members do not personally control the companies they are involved in; instead they are owned by foundations. These are very generous in their funding of research and education – the main foundation, named after the childless Knut and Alice Wallenberg, is the second-largest supporter of basic scientific research in Europe. It has grown to be worth £7.5 billion and has dished out a total of more than £2 billion during its lifetime. The guiding principle is *landsgagneligt*, which means 'benefiting the nation', which we briefly encountered in Chapter 11. 'We work our butts off in the financial part, but we do it for another reason, and that is the development of Sweden. It is how we have been brought up,' Peter Wallenberg Jr, Jacob's brother, told the *Financial Times*.

A consequence of this arrangement is that the Wallenberg family tops the rankings of the most powerful business families in Sweden, and indeed in Europe, but does not appear in rich lists. 'That is not to say that we are not doing well economically,' Jacob Wallenberg says, stating the obvious. 'But our fortunes have nothing to do with the fortunes of the foundations.' The Wallenberg sphere currently comprises the industrial holding companies Investor AB and FAM AB, their respective holdings, and 15 non-profit foundations. With dividends from the holdings, the foundations have supported research in Sweden since 1917.

'We would call that our ecosystem,' Wallenberg says. 'The idea was that it would trickle through society and eventually benefit people. What is important in the foundations is *lands-gagneligt*, which was typical of that day and age for Knut and Alice, very nationalistic and Sweden-oriented when they founded the first and biggest foundation. It means when we look at things it has to be for the good of the company, that is part of the bylaws. Hence it is an important part of our thinking.' This general line of thought is something you find not only among the Wallenbergs, but also with 'many other business owners' in Sweden, he says, adding that this is a key explanation of why the country has a disproportionate number of world-leading, high-tech companies in relation to the number of citizens. 'We are focused, we put a lot of energy into R&D, and we do this over a long time. It seems to work.'

For governments concerned that businesses should be giving back to society, and not just thinking about their own short-term interests, this must be a powerful argument. 'It is not unimportant when you ask a member of the family how they engage with politicians,' Wallenberg confirms. After all, the better the companies do, the more dividends will go to the foundations, and the more goes to Swedish research and development. 'That defines when we talk to politicians, when we engage in developing businesses, when we decide whether we should be in Sweden or elsewhere; we are partly coloured by that basic set-up, which we did not decide – it was decided for us 100 years ago, so we have to work accordingly. When I or my cousin or brother wake up in the morning, we think: the better the individual companies perform, the more dividends will go into the coffers of the foundations.'

The family businesses have also had to learn to live with, and even benefit from, strong and mostly pragmatic trade unions. Wallenberg is unapologetic in his support for this aspect of the Swedish model. We have heard this sentiment from business leaders already, but here it is from the horse's mouth:

> It is clear in my mind that a constructive relationship and dialogue with labour is conducive to the positive development of a company; you see ample evidence of this in this country. It boils down to the fact that employee representatives at the end of the day believe in market principles and the market economy. They believe that the sound development of a company is the best provider of maximum number of employment opportunities and the good of their members.

Wallenberg says that more than once he has seen trade union representatives go to a factory where they themselves used to work and tell the workers that it has to close down. 'There has to be give and take, management has to pay respect to employee views. I would argue that in this country in 95 out of 100 cases it works very well, and I think it works better than the reverse, funnily enough.' He compares it to the way that unions work in Germany, where the most important officials represent the central union and are therefore mainly concerned with the union's interests, not the company's: 'It is a completely different culture, and completely different way of working as an employee representative, and it is not conducive to the development of the company. Whereas here in Sweden, everyone most of the time is trying to get the company to work.'

There is also a 'principle of consensus', which from a British or North American point of view ought to be impossible, he adds. Comparing his banking operations internationally, 'It was so interesting to see how decisions were made in a Swedish setting, where there were long discussions, consensus was reached, and then off you go. But you empower people, this is very important.'

He continues: 'I went to my British friends, they were all standing to attention, all waiting to be given an order. That is an important part of our Swedish "bumblebee"; we have been good at modern management, empowering young people to take decisions on their own and run parts of businesses on their own – that is not a given in many other countries. I would say that is one of the reasons that Swedish companies are at least holding the pace with other companies.'

Despite the stress on continuity and the long term in the Wallenberg outlook – the family is already grooming a sixth generation of business leaders from among its ranks – Jacob Wallenberg is emphatic that the Swedish model of today is very different from that of the 1970s. In fact, he is frustrated that the country's image abroad is still so strongly linked to that period. This 'old Swedish model' was popular abroad because it was so successful, he admits. In the mid-1960s, Sweden was the world's second richest country in terms of economic output per capita. It was then at its zenith after being transformed from a very poor country before the war. Wallenberg still remembers feeling proud at school to read statistics comparing the number of telephones per capita, the number of doctors, teachers and so on, and seeing that Sweden was at the top. But the model that delivered this development contained within it the seeds of its own downfall, he argues. Sweden allowed itself to be sucked into in a 'social experiment' by Prime Minister Olof Palme and the left.

Sweden in the 1970s and '80s consumed more than it could afford but also became a highly regulated society: 'Probably the single most regulated economy outside the Iron Curtain,' according to Wallenberg. Foreigners could not buy Swedish companies, currency controls were second to Venezuela today, there was only one Rolls-Royce in the country and a handful of Porsches, the banks were tightly controlled by the government, and the chair of the Social Democratic Women's Federation – a high-profile figure – demanded a ban on satellite dishes because she feared Swedish citizens would be bamboozled by misinformation from free-market media.

The beginning of the end of this model came on 4 October 1983, when a significant protest took place from middle-class Sweden against a proposal to increase the power of government over business. 'The idea was that politicians should decide the ownership and direction of companies, which would have been basically a communistic system,' Wallenberg explains. Palme's successor in 1995 took Sweden into the European Union. 'Now comes the real shift for Sweden, where we go from being a very regulated country to one that starts to look at alternatives. Joining the common market, accepting that other forces would have a significant say, was a very, very significant shift in this country's state of mind.'

And it was not just a shift of mind. After the economic crisis of the early 1990s, Sweden underwent a blizzard of deregulation:

> We went from being the most regulated to one of the most deregulated societies among the industrialised countries. When Americans come here and talk about the Scandinavian model, the great majority of them still think about the old, very socialistic model. Today we have a very different system, which explains ultimately why the bumblebee is flying. This shift is the most fundamental part of the explanation. Without it, I am sure we would still be flying, but at a lower height.

The economic results speak for themselves. Taxes are still high, Wallenberg admits, but the scrapping of inheritance, gift and wealth taxes early this century has been a spur for entrepreneurs and creative people. In any case, he has nothing against paying high taxes: 'We still pay the third or fourth highest taxes in the world. As much as I am the archetype of a capitalist, I support the principles behind that.' Wallenberg would like to see lower taxes, to encourage 'optimal economic development'. But all the same, he stands by the principle of wealthy people paying high taxes. 'Contrary to my American friends, who ask what I have been smoking, I think it is called being affected by your environment. I support the system of taking care of people.'

* * *

By the end of the interview, Jacob Wallenberg was in a much better mood. An hour and ten minutes of explaining the world to a slow-witted foreigner had clearly cheered him up. But it was all rather 'on message' – there was nothing particularly unexpected. Until my final question, that is. Maybe after such a disciplined and polished performance, Wallenberg had relaxed a little. Or perhaps the question really did touch a nerve.

Politics is so important in terms of creating an environment for industry to thrive, I ask, so would a Wallenberg go into politics? 'We have no legitimacy,' he fires back. Despite all the wealth the family has generated for Sweden? All the jobs, all that philanthropic largesse? Surely the family's consistency over generations made it about as legitimate as you could get? Wallenberg chooses an unexpected example to illustrate his point: 'One of the most important questions we face is young unaccompanied minors, refugees, people who are almost unemployable. The labour unions refuse to accept lower wages for that particular group, we have the highest low wage in the world. The trade union federation LO refuses to change that principle because they say it will destroy the whole set-up.'

Wallenberg instead argues that you have to find a salary level where people are willing to employ people who are today unemployable, to put them to work and into education, rather than society having to pay for them in financial support. 'I find it quite revolting, frankly speaking, that we can't find a way around this,' he says. Moreover, he feels muzzled on this issue. 'I cannot as a Wallenberg stand up on this question because I cannot – given that I am a successful capitalist – be viewed as challenging the salary levels of employed Swedes. I would have zero legitimacy doing that, and it would erode my overall legitimacy. So I get stuck in a corner where I cannot move. That is just an example of why it is difficult for a Wallenberg to engage in politics.'

So Sweden's most powerful capitalist feels 'stuck in a corner' after all, forced into silence on an issue that is filling the newspapers and airwaves with heated debate. That is the flip side of strong unions, consensus, give-and-take, and a balance between labour and capital – capital needs to tread carefully on sensitive issues.

Would Jacob Wallenberg himself like a political role, I ask – like a Swedish Donald Trump? 'I think there should be much more back and forth between business and politics,' he says. 'We don't have that tradition, unlike Britain or the US, which is a great shame because it means business has a very limited understanding of politics, and vice versa. It would be great with much more of an exchange.' That sounds as close to a 'yes' as I am going to get.

Chapter 22
Disciplined Left

Everything looks small around Göran (pronounced Yerran) Persson. He is six feet tall, but also broad, built more like a boxer than a politician. Perched on a functional chair in a bland office at JKL, the PR company he joined after leaving politics, he seems too big for the room, while the coffee cups appear Lilliputian. As a government minister in the late 1980s, finance minister from 1994 to 1996, and then prime minister for the next ten years, his time in office straddles the collapse of the old Swedish model so disliked by Jacob Wallenberg, and the rise of the new one, which Persson did much to usher in. His domineering leadership helped push through unpopular reforms that played a large role in restoring the country's finances.

Surprisingly, therefore, for a prime minister of the left, he agrees with Wallenberg – in the years before the watershed of the 1990s, Sweden stacked up some major problems. 'We had a period in the 1970s and '80s when everyone got everything they wanted. There were two coalitions in parliament – one for higher spending, one for tax cuts. They worked together to destroy the public finances. It was a very destructive period. It ended in a collapse, we had to restart it.'

Strong unions were as much to blame for the crisis as anyone else, Persson admits. In fact, they were even 'part of the destruction of the Swedish system.' But they are a pillar of the model once again: 'We have given the trade unions a special role to play, and we still do, and it works. If you follow the process of wage formation, it is extremely disciplined in Sweden. We have had this as a successful concept for the past 20 years.'

In the mid-1990s, Persson went to Wall Street as Sweden's finance minister to borrow money to cover a huge hole in the public finances. The visit was traumatic, he recalls. He had to explain to bankers why Sweden had such generous unemployment insurance, why it had such high costs in the primary school system. 'To go there and do that, and realise that, if I didn't have an answer they would not lend me the money, and if they didn't lend me money I wouldn't be able to finance the welfare society – it was a terrible experience,' he says. 'So for me it was easy to say to Swedes: we must get rid of these deficits as quickly as possible. Strong public finances are extremely important if you want to maintain the model.'

The result was a series of big reforms: pensions, wages, the public sector, welfare, taxes. 'We did everything at the same time – we used the crisis. There is nothing as productive as a good crisis; we really demonstrated this during those years. We realised that if we don't do this we will not be able to defend the Swedish model. The model is not for free, we need to work to pay for it, and to work we need to export, and to export we need to be competitive. Without competitiveness, there is no Swedish model. Without the Swedish model, there is no competitiveness.'

The Swedish model itself, says Persson, helped save the Swedish model. Because of 'a relatively fair distribution of income' in the country, combined with the assumption that everyone has the right to a good education, good healthcare and a good pension paid for by taxes, people bought into the idea that big reforms were necessary – there was a sense of all being in the same boat, and everyone standing to lose if nothing was done. All the same, Persson's government felt it had to increase taxes quite dramatically for the better off. 'They had to pay, and they paid. We had very high taxes for a couple of years. We survived and we started to cut taxes after that.' The Social Democrats were paid politically for this in 2002 with re-election, he says – people could see it was working. But to be able to convince them that it was necessary, the government needed to show that there was a fair distribution of the burdens. 'That was important,' Persson continues. 'Then you are back to the fundamentals of the Swedish model, which is also an idea of fair distribution, not just of the burdens but of the results we create together.' The result is that Sweden still combines redistribution with a relatively large public sector, paid for by taxes.

In turn, redistribution has more broadly positive effects on the economy. A good education for all is not just fair,

Persson says, but is also essential for Sweden to be competitive. 'We need children and we take care of them, it is even better if they are healthy and well educated – that is the basic idea of the Swedish welfare society. It is more economically relevant now than ever before, because of the demographic situation. We cannot afford to lose anyone. Once we had a surplus of young people – we don't have that any more, even if we are in a better situation than others.'

Like other industrialised societies, Sweden's population is ageing rapidly, creating greater demands on the welfare state, with fewer taxpayers to foot the bill. Hence, in Persson's view, the importance of maintaining a high birth rate, which in turn strengthens the economic case for family-friendly polices: 'We need to support young families, to make it possible to combine a good education and a professional career with the responsibility for two or three kids.'

Look at the universities, he adds, where women students do particularly well. 'If when they graduate we tell them, "Sorry, now you have to choose: either become a mother or a professional", then we can be sure that many will become professionals and de-prioritise family life. And we know if that happens we will be in an extremely difficult situation, because a society without children is a society that will end up in stagnation.' Persson sees greater economic advantages in encouraging women to combine families and careers: societies with children have a bigger domestic market and an orientation on the future, not the past. This is part of his explanation of the Trump phenomenon in the United States: older people looking backwards to a return of something that used to be, 'making America great again', instead of looking ahead. This attitude also means searching for someone to blame, creating the potential for dangerous political priorities.

'Family-friendly policies are thus a tremendous asset,' Persson says. The future will demonstrate that gender equality is the right way to go, too. 'It's not only about women, it's about us all – it is not driven by gender, it is driven by modernity, by young adults trying to create a better life for their families. They are all more equally engaged in it than we were, not because they have to, but because they want to.'

If it isn't obvious already, Persson is bullish about the prospects for this relatively egalitarian, welfare-oriented economy that sees its people as assets, puts them to work, taxes them, and reinvests in their comfort and development, reinforcing the virtuous circle because people see they get something in return. This future-oriented attitude fosters an interest in modernity, an openness to new technologies, new methods and trends. 'It is modern, it is relevant, it is rational. If you had asked me ten years ago, I would have been much clearer that there is a threat to the model from our Conservative and Liberal parties. But that was based on the global neoliberal wave. I think the neoliberal wave has come to an end, it doesn't offer any answers to today's problems.'

On the contrary, where countries still try to practise neo-liberal polices – encouraging unbridled free-market economics in all spheres – they often result in populist responses, Persson argues: 'Ten years ago it was a threat, I don't think they would dare to go for it now. We have had so many good years that the political confrontation is not as sharp as before. People take the model for granted, more or less.'

Sweden's openness should include its attitude to immigration, Persson says, but not the 'naive policy' of opening its doors to everyone. 'You cannot have our model and then tell everyone you are welcome to come here, because our model demands that you take part in the workforce. If you do so, then you are more than welcome. The model works perfectly as long as immigrants work – then we can maintain it.' The big group of immigrants that have arrived in the past ten years are a problem, he says. Will it mean dismantling the model by cutting wages to create more jobs? 'I don't think there is support for that. We need to find new measures to do it, with the help of creating public jobs.'

Where the system is failing, he hints, is with its treatment of the elderly – the ones who built the Swedish model. 'The pension system has one minor problem – the pensions are too low. We have to solve that. But we can afford to have that discussion now.' Unless a solution is found, Persson says, the shared assumption that 'we are all in this together' will be undermined, weakening the unwritten agreement between government and the governed that if you pay into the system, it will pay out for you.

Chapter 23
Flexible Right

Anders Borg was just 38 when he took over Sweden's finances in 2006. There followed a helter-skelter ride through drastic tax cuts that would make Donald Trump blush, the global financial crash, deeply unpopular welfare reforms, an astonishing re-election to a second term on a wave of personal popularity, and finally defeat in 2014. He took credit for making Sweden 'the rock star of recovery'. Borg's trademark ponytail haircut became a familiar feature of meetings of the global elite wresting with the fallout from the 2008 crisis. But the rollercoaster had one more plunge in store: in the summer of 2017, Borg was at a party on Stockholm's archipelago where, according to the Swedish papers, he was the worse for drink and behaved offensively. As a result, he was forced to step down from some top positions, including at Swedish investment firm Kinnevik and global banking giant Citi.

When we met in Stockholm's Old Town six months later, Borg did not seem at all like yesterday's man. He had just been hired by a company developing digital robots, and had lost none of his ebullience, or indeed his zest for economics. His starting point is already familiar to us: the mess in which Sweden found itself in the 1990s. Borg recalls how he suffered an even bigger shock than Persson when he went to Wall Street in 1995 as a banking analyst – he was thrown out of an office because its occupant had just lost a lot of money, and his job, for taking an optimistic view of Sweden's prospects. Sweden had to change. For many right-wingers like Borg, everything associated with the Swedish model felt oppressive, restrictive: they called it 'GDR Sweden' – a reference to communist East Germany – and saw an over-regulated, stagnant society similar to the Eastern bloc.

But on taking power in 2006, Borg did not intend to throw the baby out with the bathwater. 'It is clear that Sweden had deep economic problems in the 1970s and '80s. But after the crisis in the 1990s we had already started to change the Swedish model quite substantially. Our thinking back in 2006 was to develop the strengths of the Swedish model.' Indeed, Borg's prime minister and closest collaborator, Fredrik Reinfeldt, talked of 'mending, not ending' welfare, and declared: 'The Swedish people want the Swedish model.' The Conservatives even rebranded themselves as a 'workers party'. Had the right tried to reclaim the Swedish model from the left? 'I think we did that, and I am very happy with that decision, I have no intention of leaving it.' The system did not require radical change, he says, and was sufficiently flexible to adapt to changing circumstances: 'We were strengthening features that were already present in the system – we reinforced the work ethic and the entrepreneurial spirit. But fundamentally the Swedish model is a very pragmatic, down-to-earth way of dealing with the tension between social cohesion and growth … a very modern way of solving the eternal conflict between equality and expansion, cohesion versus dynamism – the model is potentially one very efficient answer.'

Borg rattles off five fundamental features of Sweden's recipe for capitalism: a free-market orientation with highly unregulated markets, especially in retail, services and welfare; one of the best entrepreneurial climates in Europe; a well-functioning labour market with a unique wage-setting process delivering both stability and competitiveness; public spending that aids growth – infrastructure, education and family policies that enable women to work; and strong public finances. To this, he says, you could add cultural features such as the Lutheran work ethic, high levels of trust and transparency, and the low level of corruption, all combining to deliver economic dynamism while keeping society together. Like Jacob Wallenberg, Borg is happy with the trade unions:

> Strong unions are the partner of the worker. On the white-collar side they put resources into strategies for wage negotiations that are individual-based, providing statistics and arguments so you can go into negotiation with your boss in a good position. It is a kind of lobby for working people, which I would say is the future role for

unions anyway: today real wage increases are pretty small anyway; it is much more about work-life balance.

There are some important caveats. For smaller companies, for example, employment protection legislation is still a major obstacle; Borg says he wants to see more flexibility to hire and fire. But he is careful to state that employers should not have more freedom to sack people without accepting some responsibility for helping them to be rehired. Here he points to the importance of Sweden's 'transition system' that we looked at in Part 3, where employers pay into a central fund that helps retrain workers who lose their jobs and which gets them back into work. This system is preferable to traditional schemes to help the unemployed, Borg says. He uses Saab as an example – the Swedish car-maker was devastated by the 2008 financial crash, but most workers were back in jobs a year or two after the company closed down.

In pursuit of greater flexibility, Borg's government tried to reach a deal in the private sector where unions would win more education for people during their working lives, with companies setting aside resources to retrain workers well before there was any threat of unemployment. The idea was to reskill people in their forties and fifties, because over the next ten or 15 years the technology would be transformed. Essentially, this was a scaling up of the existing transition system, with loans and financing for adult learning, heavy subsidies for retraining foundations, and more flexible unemployment insurance. Borg met with unions 250 times, he says, offering 'a lot of money and a lot of benefits' as part of a broad negotiation on the labour market. But it fell apart. Clearly there are limits to the flexibility of the Swedish model.

That failure to rejig the labour market still haunts Borg, who lists it as a missed opportunity. Moreover, the wage levels and undersized service sector had become a headache in light of the Borg–Reinfeldt government's second main legacy – the call to 'open your hearts' to refugees. 'We overdid it', Borg says. 'It is pretty clear we could not take 160,000 in 2015 without severe tensions.' It was 'absolutely necessary' to close the borders and cut Sweden's generosity to the absolute minimum. But he defends the original premise: 'We should punch above our weight when it comes to social responsibility,' he says. Sweden stayed out of the two World Wars, and did not have the Finnish experience of being attacked by Russia. Most Swedes felt the country did too little for the Jews, by not allowing them to come here from Germany and Poland. 'The starting point should be you should do as much as you can, your spontaneous reaction should be to invite people in, and then pragmatically adapt to the new realities,' Borg says.

However, if you have migration from countries like Afghanistan, Somalia and Iraq, where education levels are low and tacit knowledge about the modern workplace is minimal, it is extremely difficult for people to adjust to the current Swedish system, Borg believes. Getting migrant unemployment down to 10 per cent is close to impossible without lowering entry-level wages, he insists: 'With the type of immigration we have had, it's pretty obvious that the Swedish labour market needs to become much more flexible.'

Borg regrets that his government's second term was not as radical as the first, and left some important business undone. The housing and the rental markets had become an urgent problem. They looked at stock options as an incentive for entrepreneurs but left it too late: 'It is a marginal reform in terms of revenues, but super important in terms of dynamism.' Meanwhile, the cost of migration would remain high because integration will continue to be slow. The political stalemate in the country, with minority governments and the far-right holding the balance of power in parliament, boded ill for attempts to make significant changes. But the problems facing Sweden today are manageable, and compared with other countries it is still in a sweet spot: 'Yes we have problems, yes we should deal with them, but it is not comparable to the 1980s and '90s.' Borg lists the strengths of the country now: the entrepreneurial climate and the high number of start-ups; the education system that produces highly skilled workers; the overall culture with the high degree of trust.

Last but not least, politicians get on well with business, and vice versa. Borg defines himself as a typically pragmatic politician who is somewhere in the middle – both a left-wing Conservative and a right-wing Social Democrat:

A unique feature is that we have a very strong relationship between the business sector and politics. Many business people interact with the Social Democrats now they are in office today, and many business people interacted with the Conservatives when we were in power. This is a small country where most people know each other, and where you normally have very open, well-functioning contacts. It is a lot easier to be pragmatic when you actually know each other, and it is much less confrontational here because people can actually relate to each other.

PART 8

MADE BY SWEDEN

Chapter 24
Reptilian

I am handed the keys inside a huge subterranean garage, like a vast museum of Volvo's past and future. Under tailored tarpaulins, or just resting moodily, historic models stand side by side with the latest beasts to roll off the production line a short distance away. And here, glowering from the shadows, is an onyx-black Volvo XC90 T6 Inscription, Volvo's premium SUV. Mine for a whole week! 'Just bring it back in one piece,' says a technician as he waves me away.

I am behind the wheel of an iconic Swedish brand. 'Made by Sweden' says the advertising slogan. But just a few years previously, Volvo had been bought by an upstart Chinese firm called Geely. After billions of investments in new components and factories, the XC90 was the company's first all-new model under its new owners. There was a great deal riding on its success. The feeling among senior Volvo executives was that they were not just launching a new model, 'they were in effect launching a new company', the *Financial Times* reported.

Within two years of its first appearance in 2014, one in five of the cars sold by Volvo was an XC90. Falling oil prices and rising driver appetite had led to a surge in global SUV sales, accounting for a quarter of cars sold by all automobile-makers across Europe. 'We have taken a step into the premium league,' Volvo announced.

Profits were up, and the XC90 was a major contributor. The XC90 is 'the ultimate proof' of the takeover's success, said Volvo's US boss. Under the new owners 'there is an eagerness to show that we are incredibly good at making cars. We are the leading ones again, we will show we can make the best cars in the world. The result is the XC90, which is beating the shit out of the competition.'

But my first impression of the car is an anti-climax. I am not a car person; I prefer a bicycle or a boat. Cars have four wheels and an engine and they get me from A to B – who cares if they are big or small, premium or Prius? I have managed most of my life without owning one at all. But here I am driving just another car, even if it's a big one. I feel self-conscious. What will the neighbours think of this ostentatious symbol of personal wealth that has suddenly appeared outside our house? What does it say about the sort of person I am? Someone with money to burn, I suppose. And a small penis. Enormous cars with darkened windows like this are driven by gangsters in Moscow, not wimpy journalists.

And then, slowly, I begin to understand. Nought to 60mph in around six seconds. It feels like I am driving a sports car the size of an armoured personnel carrier. My younger brother-in-law, who is faster and sharper than me at everything sporty, tries to race me from a standing start in his VW Polo. Within moments he is a small speck in my rear-view mirror. Other drivers appear to be scared. I begin to recognise the precise moment they see me coming up behind them – a small swerve of panic as their instinctive reaction is to get out of the way. And then they get out of the way.

I begin to feel that I own the road. I go through a red light without noticing; the car that has right of way gives a brief and half-hearted beep on his horn, it is almost apologetic. I have priority. The French consumer psychologist Clotaire Rapaille, who worked for Chrysler in the 1990s, developed an analysis of how SUVs appeal to people's most primitive instincts. Drawing on the work of Carl Jung, Rapaille divided people's reactions to a commercial product into three levels of brain activity: the cortex, for intellectual assessments; the limbic, for emotional responses; and the reptilian, which he defined as reactions based on 'survival and reproduction'. He concluded that SUVs are 'the most reptilian vehicles of all' because their imposing, even menacing, appearance appeals to people's deep-seated desires for survival and reproduction.

The 1992 Jeep Grand Cherokee was a result of Rapaille's work, as was the Dodge Ram Pickup two years later. These cars would make other motorists want to get out of your way. Rapaille said: 'My theory is the reptilian always wins. The reptilian says, "If there is a crash, I want the other guy to die." Of course, I can't say that aloud.' To Rapaille, the Hummer SUV, based on the design of a military truck, was an embodiment of Social Darwinism, sending out a clear signal: 'Don't mess with me because I can crush you.'

Sociological studies of SUV drivers show they exhibit more risky behaviour on the road, an 'SUV effect', according to which drivers violate traffic lights, don't wear seat belts and drive while using their mobile phones. Instead of making roads safer for all motorists, you make them safer for the individual motorist by placing them inside a small tank. Geographer Stephen Graham sees the SUV as an expression of a 'new urban militarism', which uses war as 'the dominant metaphor in describing the perpetual and boundless condition of urban societies – at war against drugs, against crime, against terror, against insecurity itself.'

Behind the wheel of an XC90, I feel my primitive, reptilian instincts come alive. I am a winner, a conqueror – impregnable – stronger, bigger, faster, better. In short, I have become someone I used to despise. I am burning twice as much petrol as a Prius, and the car costs more than twice as much to buy. But wow, it feels great! And not particularly 'Swedish', either: ostentatious luxury, dodgy environmental credentials, and more than a hint of macho. How did Volvo ever get away with appropriating the male gender symbol – that circle with the phallic arrow – for its corporate logo?

Nonetheless, the XC90 seems like an appropriate metaphor for the new Swedish model that emerged from the economic crisis of the 1990s. It is a victory of Swedish consensual manufacturing methods over cheap labour and orders from the top; and at the same time a victory for a Chinese entrepreneur's ruthless focus on a profitable market segment. A success for Swedish principles of safety, quality and style, yet also a triumph of hard-nosed marketing to a reptilian demographic that eschews modesty and demands luxury in spades.

From 2019, the XC90 is available only as a hybrid that runs on both batteries and petrol. Similarly, the new Swedish model of the millennium's third decade will be a hybrid, a mix of pre-1990s industrial pragmatism with the globalised realities of the 21st century. 'Made by Sweden', but by a company owned in China.

The story of Volvo is instructive because it represents an extreme clash of economic cultures in which Sweden came out on top, benefiting both the company and its Chinese owners. History has many examples of invaders adopting the cultures of the conquered rather than imposing their own ways, whether it's the Vikings converting to Christianity in Britain, or the Manchu adopting aspects of Chinese culture after the fall of the Ming dynasty. In assimilating Volvo, however, China's corporate raiders were clear from the start – they would let Swedes be Swedes, and Chinese be Chinese.

As we shall see in the next three chapters, it is also just a rollicking good story.

Chapter 25
Yank Tank

Our story begins in Östermalm, a wealthy area of downtown Stockholm. On a warm summer's night in 2007, a handful of activists slunk through the streets, each armed with a handful of mung beans. When one of these tiny hard legumes is placed inside the valve of a car tyre, and the cap partially screwed back on, the bean depresses the poppet sufficiently to make the tyre slowly deflate. The activists were targeting so-called 'city jeeps', the Swedish nickname for SUVs – those big cars that wealthy people drive, known elsewhere as Yank tanks, Chelsea tractors or mum trucks. By the end of the night, 60 of these symbols of power and status were in a state of feeble detumescence. Owners returned to find a leaflet under the windscreen wipers, which declared:

> *Your City Jeep Kills!* In the end, climate chaos will kill us all – rich and poor. This will not happen if we sharply cut our carbon dioxide emissions. Now. Not tomorrow.

Therefore we have disabled your city jeep by letting the tyres down. Because you live in a city with good public transport, you won't have any trouble getting where you need to go without your SUV.

The leaflets were signed: 'The Indians of the Asphalt Jungle'. Inspired by this action, other groups sprang up in a dozen Swedish cities; by the end of the autumn, tyres on more than 1,500 SUVs had been deflated. The campaign sparked a debate in the Swedish media and on the web. There were calls for SUV owners to arm themselves and take revenge. 'If I ever saw any of them letting down tyres I'd knock nine shades of shite out of them!' wrote one opponent. Critics claimed the activists were hypocrites who burned far more carbon dioxide when they took holidays abroad; others said they were simply jealous of people with nice cars.

The activists in turn responded that there was simply no need for these 'monster cars' that put pedestrians, cyclists and indeed the whole of humanity at risk. SUVs had only one purpose: status for their owners, they wrote in a popular newspaper. The extra tons of metal on the roads caused fuel consumption up to four times more than a fuel-efficient car, but this didn't concern the owners as they usually had a lot of money. 'Take Volvo's popular city jeep, the XC90. It costs around £40,000, weighs over two tonnes and guzzles over a litre of gasoline every 10km,' they claimed.

By taking aim at the XC90, the group were targeting the nation's flagship car-maker. Volvo was late to the SUV party

– the XC90 was its attempt to catch up with a market that was soaring in the US and beginning to take off at home in Sweden itself. For the global car industry, SUVs were proving to be one of the most effective ways to increase profits. The 1990s had seen ever bigger and more luxurious cars, tapping into growing demand. Sweden already had a reputation for having the largest and most fuel-hungry cars in Europe, partly because Swedish drivers wanted extra-safe vehicles due to the risk of collisions with moose, which frequently wander onto the roads. Also there were no tax incentives for reducing car size and fuel consumption, so the most common Swedish-made models were already relatively large.

When Volvo presented the forerunner of the XC90 at the Detroit motor show in 1997, it seemed like a natural progression from the V70XC ('cross country') version of its midsize saloon. But still the SUV seemed to sit oddly with Volvo's values. 'The target has been to find a design that is not as macho as that of many other SUV models in the segment,' said Peter Horbury, the company's chief designer. 'We prefer to talk about a masculine appearance, a design that creates a sense of security.' This was particularly important, he said, because many SUV buyers were women who liked the feeling of safety and control.

In market terms, the XC90 came not a moment too soon. SUVs made a breakthrough on the Swedish car market in 2002, the same year that the XC90 went on sale. New buyers were mostly urban and suburban dwellers, attracted by the car's associations with outdoor life and prosperity, and by the sense of safety. These had made SUVs an attractive alternative to the sports car trend set by young urban professionals in the 1980s. While the total car market in Sweden grew by a few per cent in 2002, sales of what were now called city jeeps increased substantially more.

Swedish motoring journalists were initially sceptical. They saw these big cars as dangerous to other road users, and asked why anyone actually needed a car like this when ordinary saloons would do just as well. A Volvo SUV was a contradiction, one magazine wrote: the company wanted an image based on safety, environmental concern, sportiness and slick Scandinavian design, while SUVs were intrinsically 'dangerous, thirsty and heavy'. Sweden's fleet of vehicles was already 'worst in class' in terms of carbon-dioxide emissions when compared with the rest of Europe, a member of the Road Safety Council complained. A so-called 'penalty tax on city jeeps' was debated in parliament and the media.

The Indians of the Asphalt Jungle seem today like a rather gentle, Swedish response to a very Swedish dilemma – the nation's car-maker was caught up in a global trend that played to the country's historical preferences for big cars but clashed with its growing self-image as green and responsible. It was Scandi direct action in which nobody was hurt and nothing was damaged, no windscreens smashed or paintwork scratched, an attempt to start a debate rather than physically block the streets or destroy the enemy. The activists called off their protests after a few months, citing a dip in SUV sales but also the risk that drivers were setting off without noticing that a tyre was flat, with the potential for accidents.

In fact, much bigger forces were about to hit demand for SUVs in Sweden and around the world. The financial crisis of 2008 smashed into the global car market like a bull moose hitting a Fiat Panda. But even as sales deflated like the tyres of a Yank tank on a narrow Östermalm street, far away in Beijing a wealthy entrepreneur was planning an audacious bid for Volvo that would relaunch the XC90 as the saviour of Sweden's car industry.

Chapter 26
National Treasure

Li Shufu was accustomed to thinking big and winning difficult arguments. Born into a farmer's family near Shanghai, he went straight from school into business in 1984 with a tiny sum from his father. By the age of 21, he owned a factory making refrigerator components, the start of his own Geely brand.

In the mid-1990s, expensive imported motorcycles became popular in China, and Li somehow persuaded the government to let him bail out a struggling, state-owned motorcycle factory in Hangzhou. Before long, Geely motorcycles were being sold in 22 countries, including the US and Europe, and were China's top international brand. Just three years later, having overcome opposition from all quarters, Li became China's first private producer of motorcars. At one point, according to the *China Daily*, he begged an official: 'Please let me try. It is my dream. I'll pay for everything and take all the risks. Just give me an opportunity to win or lose on my own.' At the turn of the millennium, sales of Geely compact cars

began to take off in China and abroad. In 2006, Geely established a joint venture in Shanghai to manufacture London's
iconic black taxicab.

But Li had even bigger fish to fry. He believed that Volvo
could give him the innovation, branding and technology he
needed to propel Geely, and China's auto industry in general,
into global markets. Volvo at the time was owned by Ford, the
US multinational. Li began courting Ford's leadership, but
Geely was both a novice and a minnow: in 2005 its sales were
just 140,000 at the lower end of the market, while Ford was
selling more than 6 million cars a year. At the Detroit auto show
in 2008, Li met a senior Ford executive who was courteous
but appeared put off by Geely's size.

Just a few months later, however, the global financial crisis
struck, giving Li an opportunity that would, in his words, be
like 'a world-famous movie star marrying a Chinese peasant'.
In February, the news broke that Geely was preparing to bid
for Volvo, and that Ford was keen to offload its loss-making
Nordic subsidiary to focus on the crisis in its home market.
A summer of speculation was followed by an autumn of
Swedish contempt and outrage, as it emerged that Geely was
the front-runner to take over their national treasure. Most of
the Swedish media was caustic, with a great deal of scepticism
that an unknown rickshaw of a company could save this sleek
Scandinavian limousine with 80 years of history behind it.

Geely's acquisition was presented as damaging or even
dangerous, with dire predictions of the collapse of the Volvo
brand, the closure of its mighty Torslanda plant in Gothenburg,

the loss of technology to China, and mass unemployment for Volvo employees and subcontractors on Sweden's west coast. It seemed impossible that Western and Chinese company cultures could successfully combine. 'The Chinese car industry is primitive and has nothing to teach Volvo,' sneered one newspaper's motoring columnist. 'Unless it's about how to deal with unions – the communist dictatorship does not allow a free trade union movement.' Another wrote: 'Geely can kill Volvo's strengths. … There is only one plus: the ability for Volvo to grow rapidly in China. The uncertainties and risks are far greater.'

A major fear was that the Chinese would steal technological secrets – a concern fuelled when Geely exhibited what looked like a replica Rolls-Royce Phantom at the Shanghai auto show in April 2009. Volvo's unions said they were worried that subcontractors would stop selling Volvo the latest technology, fearing it would be stolen, leading to a loss of competitiveness and jobs. The relationship between Volvo and its suppliers was a long-term partnership based on trust, argued Magnus Sundemo, head of the engineers' trade union at Volvo. Geely was a different animal, hiding its ownership structure behind unlisted companies in the Cayman Islands. 'It's scary,' he said.

Sundemo, a soft-spoken man with a Tiggerish smile, became a tireless agitator against a Geely takeover. 'I was one of the biggest opponents of the Chinese, I was out in the media and TV and all over the place, talking about the risk of this company just making copycats of Western cars,'

Sundemo recalls, shortly after his retirement from Volvo's board. What could they add or bring to the table? 'I was scared that the suppliers would disappear when they understood they would be doing business with a Chinese company. There were good opportunities to grow in China without being owned by the Chinese.'

For these reasons, Volvo's owners should be based in the Nordic region – they should be people who understood 'the Volvo spirit' and its vision of cars with high environmental and safety performance. The engineers' union called on the government to step in and find a Nordic owner. Sundemo took the initiative to create a rival Swedish consortium to challenge Geely. Consortium Jakob, named after Volvo's first-ever model in 1927, was fronted by Sören Gyll, a former boss of Volvo Group in the years before the company was divided and its automobile division sold to Ford in 1999. Gyll had used his influence on Volvo's board in the early 1990s to prevent a merger with French car-maker Renault. The workers had wanted to keep Volvo Swedish, Gyll said.

Consortium Jakob called on the company's workers to become part-owners by chipping in two months' wages. Swedish car dealers were also offered shares. Magnus Sundemo recalls: 'We went around all the rich people in Sweden to ask for support. If we had gone to the Swedish public we could have raised the money – I got a lot of letters of support from all over Sweden at the time. But none of the politicians believed in us. They had been through the docks crisis in the 1970s when the shipbuilders went down, the government had stepped in and it was a disaster.

They didn't want to do that again. So we weren't able to raise enough money.'

Already, however, attitudes among those closest to Geely had begun to change. The blue-collar workers' union IF Metall was led at the time by Stefan Löfven, who five years later would become Sweden's prime minister. In the early autumn of 2009, just as Consortium Jakob was unravelling and the dream of a Swedish buyout was falling apart, Löfven signalled a more positive attitude. His union was in touch with Geely, which understood the Swedish model, he told newspapers: 'We are careful to emphasise that, to succeed, you must have good contacts with the employees so that they get a high level of participation. [In this way] the Swedish model gives a competitive edge. Geely says that they understand this, and that when production takes place in Sweden, it must be done on the terms that apply here. We naturally want to develop that reasoning.' What Löfven took from his discussions with the Chinese was that production and development would remain in Sweden. 'They see the value of Swedishness, which has to start in Sweden.'

Sundemo and his engineers also met with Geely's top management. It was an open meeting, Sundemo said at the time, during which they got some answers. Li told them he was listening to the union. 'It felt good,' Sundemo said. Now he himself was beginning to feel the heat: his insistence on Swedish ownership had attracted accusations of xenophobia towards the Chinese, and he was forced to explain himself. Increasingly it looked as though Geely would win the bidding war and become Volvo's new owner. Sundemo tells me: 'I was in a critical position. People were asking: "Will I resign?" But we visited China and met Li Shufu. I said to him: "We both have something in common, we both love the company." Li asked if I would support the takeover – otherwise he wouldn't go ahead. There had been serious problems in South Korea when the Chinese did a takeover, maybe he didn't want to repeat that. Then he told us about his plans for "freeing the tiger" at Volvo.'

Li was known for a poetic choice of words. Sundemo was not the first to hear him describe Volvo as a 'tiger' that he wanted to set free. 'Free the tiger? I thought it was bullshit at the time,' Sundemo says. 'I didn't understand at all what he meant. But he saw the strength in the organisation. He took a tremendous risk when he bought Volvo.' When the deal went through the following year, Li vowed to respect Volvo's independence. He promised the workforce that he would preserve Volvo's big operations in Europe's high-cost, low-growth car market, arguing that growth in China would allow Geely to save jobs in areas such as research and development.

'Geely is Geely and Volvo is Volvo,' Li said. 'We should not be characterised as father and son, rather as brothers, and we want to benefit from each other's strengths.' Later, he told the *Financial Times*: 'We gave them back their freedom.'

Chapter 27
Freeing the Tiger

At the time, Geely's purchase of Volvo from Ford in 2010 was one of the most high-profile takeovers by corporate China, and it still serves as a test case for Beijing's industrial ambitions. The deal is part of the debate that rages over China's overseas acquisitions, which are often subject to close European and US scrutiny. At the higher levels inside Volvo itself there was an acute sense of the company's vulnerability. What happened, however, came as a surprise to everyone.

'I believe that when Geely acquired Volvo they did so for the brand, the technology, the engineering, the market presence. The one thing they had – and that was misunderstood by many – was a huge respect for Swedish innovation, engineering, people and the Swedish business model,' says Tom Johnstone (who we met in Chapter 15), one of the European corporate heavyweights brought in by Geely to help steer the ship. Although a Scot, Johnstone is a veteran of Swedish industry, the former boss of ball-bearing maker SKF and with a string of Swedish board positions under his belt. All its life, Volvo cars had been a division of a bigger industrial group – first as part of Volvo AB, which made trucks, earth-movers and marine engines, and then a division of Ford. Now it became a company in its own right, giving it a shot of energy.

Ford had brought some financial discipline, but it wanted Volvo to be part of the bigger structure, says Lex Kerssemakers, the Dutch head of Volvo in the US who, when we spoke in 2017, had been with the company for 25 years. Volvo management felt under siege by the Americans: 'Engineers and people here felt limited in their freedom, we had to comply with rules not based on our values and ethics – instead, there was hierarchy, processes, law and order, meetings, formalities. Swedes want to be independent, they want to be left alone, they don't bother other people too much. When you take away their independence they start to revolt, and that happened a little under Ford.'

The Chinese were clever, Kerssemakers says – the new owners didn't start a revolution, but created momentum: 'That was a huge difference, it triggered a lot of dynamism. Follow your business guts, they said.' Geely gained a lot of respect because they trusted Volvo, they had the patience and vision to allow the company to do its job. 'We know how to make cars, the competence level is extremely high, so the Chinese said: you are the knowledgeable partner. What they brought was an entrepreneurial attitude – follow your intuition, don't try to calculate everything. Many of us felt extremely obliged not to disappoint the major shareholder.'

Under Ford, Volvo had adopted a tortoise approach – 'withdraw into your shell, pull in your legs and head and allow the Ford strategy to wash over you,' says Carl-Peter Forster, a German executive who had worked in the auto industry all over the world, helping to lead companies such as BMW, General Motors and Tata Motors before he joined Volvo. 'The American automotive companies believe it is best to tell everyone exactly what process to follow every day. So you push back. I think Volvo has started sticking arms and legs out and is moving forward confidently again. Geely supported us financially, but didn't rescue us – that changed the mindset inside the organisation. You have to allow the organisation to build a great product, and allow the people to decide what is a great product that suits our brand.'

The approach was similar to that of the new Indian owners who took over Jaguar Land Rover at around the same time that Geely bought Volvo, Forster says. A more entrepreneurial culture came in and said: I believe in the brand, lets unleash the organisation. 'Initially you have to fund it, but in both cases it worked. It was a huge investment for Geely, and they are a smashing hit.' The Chinese owners were not benevolent, it was all about business performance, about moving faster and growing, being more entrepreneurial, about drive and speed: 'We didn't have that under Ford – how could we? We were told which model we could do.'

This was what 'freeing the tiger' looked like in practice. 'Li Shufu is pushing like hell – we will never be going fast enough for him,' says Johnstone. 'It's a lesson for the rest of Sweden

– we need to go faster. Those companies who are open to Chinese competition already realise that. … The Chinese can build a city for 10 million people in the time it takes for us to build a bridge.'

Magnus Sundemo, the union leader and arch-sceptic of the Chinese, now admits that his fears were groundless. When Geely first took over and were making changes at the top, they sacked a lot of managers – with Sundemo's assistance. 'I didn't tell them who to sack, but I advised them. In a sense, that was the Swedish model,' he says. Sundemo remembers the first board meeting under the new boss, when Li started reciting poetry: 'It was both exciting and scary. They came in with a philosophy of handing control back to Volvo. That was a brave step.' Geely gave the top management freedom to do what they wanted, and they were supportive, instead of scrutinising every decision as Ford did. 'Ford put in controllers, a mega matrix organisation. They had all these managers in human resources, research, production and finance, to interfere in the organisation. Ford had a lot of cash to throw around, but no ideas about how to develop the industry.'

It seemed freeing the tiger might be more than a catchy slogan. The Chinese strategy of running Volvo Cars as an independent organisation within Geely, with unprecedented freedom and access to capital, delivered results. After an initial slump in 2011–12, Volvo rebounded. Its profit margins nudged up towards those of the big three German brands that are seen as Volvo's main competitors – Audi, BMW and Mercedes. Sales hit a record at more than half a million cars in 2015, and continued to climb. Its first new models under Chinese ownership were well reviewed. Development times were slashed – it took Volvo 44 months to develop a new car in 2010; five years later it was down to 30 months. Instead of extracting a dividend, Geely invested all the cash back into the business, spending £7bn on developing new models, engines and platforms.

Before the Chinese takeover, Volvo had no manufacturing facilities outside Europe; now it has three plants in China and one in the US, while China has become its biggest market. Its new R&D company, CEVT, went from zero to more than 2,000 highly skilled employees in Gothenburg in the blink of an eye, bringing together an international team of designers. 'The suspicious view [of the Chinese] gradually disappeared,' Christer Karlsson, professor at Copenhagen Business School, told the *Financial Times*. Sundemo says: 'We could never have made the investments that were made under Geely if we had remained under Ford. At no time did we come close to expanding so fast and taking such brave decisions on new products.' In the words of Hans Enocson, former chief executive of GE in Sweden: 'Ford didn't invest in Volvo, they just milked it.' Geely was a very different owner.

The most tangible result of the takeover, the XC90, bore little relation to the old Volvo SUVs whose tyres were deflated by environmentalists ten years earlier. This was a second generation SUV, redesigned from top to bottom, the quintessential product of Chinese energy combined with Swedish expertise. 'The XC90 is Swedish,' Sundemo insists. 'Our big idea was to build on the history, the good things – safety, environmental quality, Nordic design, and to go the full way.' Indeed, the new model emerged out of a tension between Volvo's Chinese and Swedish leaderships. In 2013, Li publicly criticised Volvo's design, particularly interiors that he saw as 'too Scandinavian'. Sundemo recalls: 'In the beginning there were some misunderstandings – Li wanted to go luxury, Jacoby wanted to be Nordic.'

Carl-Peter Forster also noted this contrast: 'It is quite interesting to observe – to create a Swedish super-premium international brand entails some interesting challenges. One of the slight challenges we have is to present the premium-ness of Volvo in a country like China, where premium-ness is all to do with visual richness, gold-plated things – which is absolutely un-Swedish. Lots of people love the restrained, minimal Swedish design using natural colours. For certain luxury brands that is difficult. Lots of Europeans have a soft spot for this refined luxury that has a sense of understatement and style. Not to the same extent in Asia or Russia.'

It could be tempting to see Geely and Volvo as a story of happily ever after. This tectonic shift in the Swedish and Chinese business landscape might seem to have taken place largely without tremors, eruptions or earthquakes. This is not the case. Cars are a cut-throat business. Throats were cut. Li sacked his first appointed chief executive, Stephan Jacoby, in 2012 while the latter was still in hospital after suffering a stroke. Jacoby was popular with staff for his love of cars and reluctance to allow Geely to get its hands on too much Swedish technology. Pehr G. Gyllenhammar, a former head of Volvo Group, recently described Volvo's fate as a tragedy. 'I think they've ruined the whole of Volvo since I left, dismantled the largest industry in Sweden in a hurry, without getting anything for it. ... There are many who are extremely pleased, but not the Swedish people, who have enormous loyalty.'

The changes have been part of a gradual decay of the Swedish model, according to Glenn Bergström, head of the blue-collar union at Torslanda. To him, the fate of nearby Saab still hangs over Volvo like a shadow. Hit by the same crisis that drove Ford to sell Volvo to the Chinese, Saab failed to find a buyer with deep enough pockets and went bankrupt in 2011. Thousands of jobs were lost. 'We didn't used to fear unemployment, now we do,' Bergström says. 'If something should happen to Volvo Cars there is not a chance in hell that they could take care of that.'

So how does the story look from the Chinese side? At the time of the acquisition, the media were fond of quoting a Chinese expression that Geely buying Volvo was 'like a snake swallowing an elephant'. The simile referred to the differences in size between the two companies, rather than any anthropomorphic features of the animals in question. But after the event, the phrase seems more appropriate as an image of an elephant-shaped snake, its thin skin stretched over something that is still clearly an elephant.

In his simple, oak-panelled office at Volvo's low-ceilinged headquarters in Torslanda, Peter Zhang, who played a key role in Geely's takeover of Volvo and was Li Shufu's spokesperson, takes a big-picture view of the process. Despite the high costs, there was no question of closing production and moving it to China. It is more about generating value, he says: 'The costs going forward will level out – through productivity gains, higher levels of automation and so on. It has turned out to be good. We didn't even think of reducing the manufacturing footprint in Sweden in 2010, and there is even less reason to think about that now.' For Zhang, companies are just organisations of people, and those people have roots – they have been brought up in their own ways, immersed in their own cultures. 'So it's all about how you have a company style or culture that brings the best out of people.'

Of course there were culture clashes – this was inevitable, Zhang says. But Li Shufu was a 'sensible guy' who had respect for Volvo's culture and core values, and he established a governance structure so Volvo was governed by an independent board. Zhang says: 'When we took over in the beginning we said Volvo will be governed independently. "Geely is Geely, Volvo is Volvo" – that was the catchphrase. So the board has been trusted to make decisions with the support of the owner. We have had a lot of strategic projects between Geely and Volvo, with people working together, so I have overheard comments about the other organisations, and people might feel a little frustrated when it comes to understanding each other. But these sorts of tensions over time have become fewer and fewer, people are trying to find ways to understand each other and work with each other.'

Zhang met the former union boss Stefan Löfven once more after Löfven had become prime minister in 2014. 'When we saw him again he was very pleased,' Zhang recalled. 'He said we had delivered what we promised.'

PART 9

GOING GREEN

Chapter 28
Toxic

Sweden has a dirty little secret. For decades, it has been dumping toxic waste in a hole on Langøya, a tiny island off the coast of Norway. That hole is now full. The company that runs it started looking for somewhere else where it could dispose of the toxins produced by Swedish incinerators. It zeroed in on Brevik, a little village south of the capital, Oslo. For more than a century, a local cement factory had been digging limestone beneath the town, creating 300km of tunnels. These could now be stuffed with the nasty stuff.

Since the 1990s, Langøya has been the final resting place for most of the toxic fly ash produced by burning household waste in Sweden. The island has capacity for 10 million cubic metres, but by 2022 it will start to overflow. NOAH, the company behind the landfill, looked at a hundred alternative sites across the country and narrowed it down to three, of which Brevik was the most attractive. NOAH imports a quarter of a million tonnes of fly ash annually from Swedish and Danish incinerators, mixing it with waste from other industries. The company reckoned that, once Langøya was full, the Brevik site could operate for 30 or 40 years.

The locals were not happy. From being an idyllic summer destination, Brevik would become known as a toxic rubbish dump. They cited expert opinion that the waste treatment plant nearby would handle dangerous gases and acid, just a few hundred metres from people's homes. Moreover, simply disposing of the waste meant ignoring new technologies with the potential to clean up the fly ash and neutralise its toxicity altogether. NOAH countered that no other method made commercial or environmental sense. At the time this book went to print, the debate was still in full swing.

It is ironic that Norway's toxic hot potato should have arisen from a Swedish environmental success. After it banned dumping waste in landfill in 2005, Sweden began to burn increasing amounts of garbage, both household and industrial, generating heat and power while slashing its greenhouse gas emissions. The process was so smooth and efficient that countries such as the UK paid to offload their waste onto Sweden, prompting awestruck speculation in foreign media that the country had 'run out of rubbish' and was forced to import it. In 2017, about a fifth of the rubbish consumed by Sweden's 34 waste-to-energy plants came from abroad.

Incineration is no longer controversial in Sweden, because it is clean. After Swedish scientists in the 1980s studied the release of dioxins – dangerous mutagens and carcinogens – from municipal incinerators, strict requirements were introduced for cleaning up the process. The amount of waste burned for energy grew fourfold in 30 years, but total dioxin emissions *fell* by 99 per cent. Power companies boasted that their only emissions were water vapour. It was almost too good to be true. Like a small intestine for society, incinerators digested the detritus of modern life, extracting every last drop of usefulness and turning it into energy.

But the intestine still had to poop. And Sweden sent the poop to Norway. Yet the hype about Sweden's smart way of dealing with rubbish has been immense. Here is James Corden on the popular *Late Show* on US television in late 2016:

> Guys, this is going to blow your mind. In Sweden, they burn waste in gigantic, state-of-the-art recycling plants and use that energy for heat. It's really cool but there's one problem. They've run out of trash and they're having to import it from other countries. So to keep their economy running, they have to import trash. Sweden is amazing, it's incredible. The people are beautiful, they have no trash, nothing bad ever happens there. The worst thing to happen to that entire country is when the band ABBA broke up.

You don't need James Corden to tell you that, outside its borders, Sweden has an exceptionally good reputation on the environment. The biggest international story to come out of Sweden in 2018 was 'plogging', billed as a Swedish fitness craze for jogging while picking up rubbish, which added to the hype. 'If there's a paradise for environmentalists, this Nordic nation must be it,' a French journalist wrote recently. When you try to unpack the reasons for this, however, the question 'Where's the poop?' keeps nagging away.

Part of the problem is untangling the measures that really make a difference from those that just sound nice, but frankly are fluffy and ineffectual. Janey Mehks is Stockholm's business development manager for 'cleantech'. Cleantech, she explains, is any technology that is better for the environment than existing technology. 'So everything, basically.' Mehks can point to all sorts of initiatives that come under the cleantech rubric – shared car services, green development zones, the world's first urban biochar carbon sink, rooftop agriculture, automated vacuum waste collection – but which of these are significant, and which are cute but little more than good PR? It is all presented as clever, new, innovative and sustainable, often with a slick video featuring a breathless narrator, upbeat music and images of smiling children. But where's the poop?

Swedes are not genetically nicer or cleaner than any other people, yet when it comes to their greenness, there tends to be a simplistic emphasis on the positive. 'People's environmental awareness is higher here,' says Mehks. 'We are close to the archipelago and nature, people go into the countryside at the weekends.' You don't need to be a dyed-in-the-wool climate sceptic to find statements like this unconvincing. A group of foreign students in Stockholm in 2018 were treated to a boat tour of the archipelago along with a speaker on 'Sweden's interaction with nature and how that informs our business philosophy'. Who did they think they were kidding?

In some respects, greenness comes easy for a country with no fossil fuel reserves, lots of wide, open spaces and a temperate climate. More than half of the energy Sweden generates is from renewable sources, of which the lion's share is hydropower. This puts it ahead of the rest of the EU, although behind Norway and Iceland. Sweden also has abundant forests, creating a renewable supply of biomass as fuel. And it is cold up north, attracting energy-intensive industries such as data centres, which use the low temperature as free cooling for their vast arrays of computers. In 2018, Facebook announced it would double the size of its data centres in Luleå, near the Arctic Circle, attracted by the cold, cheap hydropower and tax breaks. At the time of the announcement, Facebook was already consuming more than 1 per cent of Sweden's total energy production, a proportion set to double with the expansion. Facebook is not alone – Stockholm receives inquiries from data-centre companies almost every week, says Mehks.

When it comes to incineration, the country has been well served by the old Swedish model. District heating – where a central boiler supplies heat to many homes – spread rapidly in Sweden in the 1960s, consistent with a prevailing acceptance of centralised, community-wide solutions to social issues at the time. While centralised heating systems involve inevitable heat losses and big initial investments, there were also many advantages: cheap oil could be used to fire the boilers; large, centralised heating plants were efficient to maintain and could also generate electricity – so-called combined heat and power; surplus heat from industry, and everything from data centres to shops, could be fed into the system. And it was much easier to control emissions from a few large power plants than tens of thousands of local or domestic heating systems. As a result, about half of Sweden's homes are heated by district heating systems, and in Stockholm it is 80 per cent.

When concerns began to grow about greenhouse gas emissions, it was then relatively easy to switch to burning biomass and household or industrial waste in the district heating boilers. Crucially, the revenue from selling heat and power is sufficient to allow operators to make a suitable profit, despite the high cost of cleaning toxins from the emissions. District heating was an integral part of the *folkhemmet* – the people's home promised by the Swedish model in its earlier incarnation (see Chapter 16) – and 'one of the main reasons that Sweden performs so well on the environment,' says Fortum, a Finnish energy company that runs several combined heat and power stations in Sweden.

Sweden has also benefited from some good timing and bold moves on the environment, helping to form its reputation as a world leader on this issue. In 1968, the Swedish government proposed that the United Nations hold its first summit on the environment, which it did in Stockholm in 1972, marking a turning point in global green politics and putting sustainability on the UN's agenda. The Stockholm Conference, as it came to be known, threw down a marker for the rest of the world. In 1991, Sweden became one of the first countries to tax carbon, gradually raising its levy to be the highest in the world. The tax has helped the country cut greenhouse gas emissions by a quarter even while the economy has grown by 60 per cent – it has 'decoupled' from emissions, to use the jargon. A tax on nitrogen oxide emissions from power plants, introduced in 1992, saw emissions decline by 50 per cent per unit of energy produced. In 2010, Stockholm became the first city to be named 'the green capital of Europe', thanks to its efforts on noise pollution, cleaner water, waste disposal and open spaces. It gave the city a marketing boost and created a new surge of interest around Sweden's green credentials.

At the UN's climate change conference in Paris in 2015, countries agreed to try to keep the increase in global average temperatures to below 2 degrees Celsius above pre-industrial levels. This spurred another eye-catching initiative in Stockholm, where left and right agreed that the country should aim to have zero carbon emissions by 2045. Shortly after, Sweden became the first country to legislate to be 'climate neutral' before the mid-point of the century. Stockholm aimed to reach the target even earlier.

Chapter 29
Goals

Sweden's climate agreement, with its aim of turning the country 'carbon neutral' by 2045, breaks the pattern of short-termism in global economics. So says Anders Wijkman, a senior centre-right figure and co-president of the Club of Rome, a high-level think tank on sustainability. Wijkman chaired the group of Swedish political and business leaders who came up with the 2045 target. On the summer's day in 2017 when Sweden's parliament passed the target into law, Wijkman stood back to look at its historical significance: 'I dare to say this is due to both a long-term perspective and broad political backing,' he wrote. Shortly afterwards, he and his other Club of Rome co-president launched a blistering attack on short-term thinking in free-market economies, and its impact on the environment:

> Since the 1980s, capitalism has moved from furthering
> the economic development of countries, regions and the

world towards maximising profits, and then to a large extent profits from speculation. In addition, the capitalism unleashed since 1980 in the Anglo-Saxon world, and since 1990 worldwide, is mainly financial, supported by excessive deregulation and liberalisation of the economy. The term 'shareholder value' popped up in the business pages of the media worldwide, as if that was now the new epiphany and guardrail for all economic action. In reality, it served to narrow business down to short-term gains, often at the expense of social and ecological values.

There seems to be a strong echo here of the long-term outlook of Swedish business that we encountered in Part 4. Of course, it would be silly to suggest there is a direct link between the dual-share structure of Swedish company ownership and the 2045 carbon goal. But the fact is that Wijkman and politicians of left and right sat down to debate climate change with business leaders accustomed to thinking about the longer term, not just next week's share price. There were divisions among business leaders on climate issues, Wijkman says. But by including two business groups on the committee, they competed to outdo each other, neither wanting to be seen to be the climate bad guy.

Short-term incentives are needed to reward long-term action, Wijkman says. Not far to the north of Östermalm in Stockholm is an experiment in matching the short- and long-term interests of construction companies in order to radically reduce carbon emissions from housing. The city administration is investing about £1.7 billion over 25 years to develop a former industrial site, used previously for gas and oil depots, which now enjoys the breathless title of the Royal Stockholm Seaport. This is a large-scale trial of green city living. It has some fluffy stuff – like tunnels under the roads to prevent wandering frogs being crushed by SUVs. And it has some gimmicky, gee-whiz features – like a vacuum waste collection system, where the contents of all the rubbish bins are sucked underground into a network of pipes several times a day. This at least has the benefit that the area needs fewer garbage trucks on its streets.

Most importantly, however, the city has imposed a strict limit on energy consumption for homes in this area – half the legal limit elsewhere in the city – and is making this progressively stricter while scoring all buildings on a range of sustainability measures, including longevity. When land is put out for tender, the better a company scores on these measures, the more chance it has of winning the contract. So far around 50 construction companies have signed up to these conditions and built apartment blocks in the area. In return, they get to work with university research departments and high-tech companies to experiment with green urban design.

The homes are sold or rented commercially, with prices around the same as any new apartments in central Stockholm – in other words, they are pricey. But there is a high demand for apartments in this location. All the same, because of the environmental requirements, companies don't make the same profits as they would elsewhere. This is a shop window for them and an opportunity to try out new design methods.

Legislation in Sweden, and Europe as a whole, is slowly driving down energy consumption. 'By learning how to build low-energy buildings they are ahead of the competition, it is an investment for them,' says Bo Hallqvist of the city development administration. 'Housing is a conservative business, money talks every minute – we are trying to change the business model here.' There is a lot of learning involved, he says. Stockhom has 'a 100-year perspective' – these are not buildings that you will have to knock down in 40 years. Anyone can build a single block with high sustainability, but here they are learning to do this on a large scale. 'When we can show we can build a lot of houses to this level of quality and environmental efficiency, then the city can decide to do the same across Stockholm. We are looking at what we can achieve for the long term,' Hallqvist says. As a result of this process, Stockholm has insisted that all new construction on land earmarked for development by the city must now meet the energy consumption limits set by the Royal Stockholm Seaport. This level will be progressively reduced as the city nears its carbon-free goal.

Since the Seaport project began, the city administration has changed hands twice from left to right, and back again. But this has not affected progress, pointing to a second feature of the new Swedish model that we have encountered earlier in the book – the importance of consensus. Hallqvist explains: 'An important thing in Sweden is that we work with consensus all the time. We don't start major projects until all the major parties agree – we cannot afford for changes in political leadership to affect them.' Wijkman describes this process at work on the committee that established the 2045 zero carbon target: 'In Sweden for almost a century now we have had coalition governments of the centre-left and -right. In the climate debate neither bloc wanted the other to emerge as the more radical. There was an eagerness to agree that this is the type of issue that is beneficial for society, but also for the parties themselves – to avoid constant bickering about targets and details. There were certain issues where I felt there was even an eagerness on the centre-right and -left to have a broad agreement, because they didn't want to be seen to be less ambitious than the other side.'

One foreign company that appreciates the advantages of consensus on the environment is Northvolt, a start-up founded by two former executives of Tesla, the pioneer of electric cars in the US. Northvolt has plans to build Europe's largest factory for lithium-ion batteries, at a cost of £3bn, aiming to start large-scale production by 2020. The company was attracted to Sweden by clean, cheap energy, the proximity of key minerals in the Nordics and the presence of academic expertise in battery production. But there was another aspect, according to Paolo Cerruti, Northvolt's Italian chief operating officer: 'One of the major advantages of Sweden for doing business is the relative stability and common sense that politicians apply in this country.' When administration B arrives in power, it will not scratch everything that administration A did, saying these guys are a bunch of jokers and this should never have happened. 'Which is basically what the US did when Obama left power,' Cerruti says. 'This gives us a lot of confidence. If it is the right thing to do, they will support it, they will do it, regardless of who is in power. This gives visibility, stability, it is a pitch point for investors, especially non-Nordic investors.'

As the company sought to try out its concept and create a blueprint that could be replicated elsewhere, the local consensus on the environment helped it decide to build its first factory in Sweden. 'This is probably one of the easiest places where we can do it, then we can replicate that much more easily around Europe,' Cerruti says. Strict regulation of the economy was an entry barrier for Northvolt, he says, but setting the bar high in regulatory terms forces companies to focus on efficiency and automation, 'rather than just having a bunch of workers hammering away'. This harks back to a feature of the Swedish economy that we encountered in Part 3 – the system of relatively high wages forces companies to raise productivity by using the latest techniques, rather than driving down the price of labour. In the same way, a strict regulatory environment can be a spur for innovation, rather than just a drag on competitiveness.

Björn Hugosson, head of the climate unit at Stockholm's city hall, had a similar experience when he tried to encourage greener transport in the city, by persuading private companies to use cars run on ethanol. He encountered surprisingly little resistance: 'They said: we want long-term rules. If you provide us with the rules and strategy and tell us this will last for 20 years, as long as it is fair and is the same for anybody, then we can adapt.'

Stockholm has also been successful in converting a quarter of its buses to biogas, a byproduct of human sewage. In a move that gives a rather different connotation to the question 'Where's the poop?', in 2006 the Stockholm county administration agreed to buy all the biogas produced by the municipal water company for the next 20 years. This long-term agreement between two public bodies created the stability of demand necessary for private companies to step in and clean up the gas, making fuel for buses. The city has also developed a fleet of taxis running on ethanol and biogas. Despite these successes, transport is a headache for Hugosson. Use of private cars is soaring in and around the capital, driven by trends in leisure and shopping.

Moreover, neither the city's zero-carbon target nor the nation's includes the vast amounts of carbon generated by manufacturing goods *outside* Sweden and transporting them into the country. The impact of consumption on the climate doesn't show up in the zero-carbon calculation, even though in this respect a Swede is just as polluting as any other European citizen, if not more so, because of their high levels of personal consumption. In this respect, the 2045 zero-carbon target sets the goalposts quite far apart: you can hardly fail to score, even if you are kicking from the other end of the pitch.

'Zero emissions' does not mean that in 2045 Sweden won't emit any greenhouse gases – the Climate Act commits the country to reduce its absolute emissions by 85 per cent below the level it had back in 1990. It plans to offset its remaining emissions by investing in projects that contribute to reducing pollution elsewhere. Taking these factors into account, Wijkman tells me, Sweden's emissions target should be at least twice as ambitious.

A transformation of capitalism on that scale has barely begun: 'Even if our proposals can be as relatively ambitious, they are not ambitious enough.'

Inside Sweden's Environmental Protection Agency, Hans Wrådhe looks like the very essence of an environmental scientist – a warm and friendly face, earnest spectacles and a T-shirt from a holiday to Dubrovnik that clearly took place several years ago. Wrådhe is responsible for checking Sweden's progress towards hitting its green targets. Does Sweden deserve its reputation as a front-runner on climate change and the environment?

> Sweden is special in that we are the first country that has a Climate Act and a clear goal to become climate neutral. But in terms of consumption, we are not an ideal country. We have quite a lot to do ourselves before we tell others to be better.

Chapter 30
Green Shoots

It might not seem very logical to include a chapter on 'start-ups' in a discussion of Sweden's green ambitions – there is nothing intrinsically green about starting a business. On the other hand, start-ups are associated with bringing new ideas to bear on solving difficult problems. If we want to innovate ourselves out of a climate crisis, then it becomes imperative to be able to turn ideas into solutions that make economic sense. And in this respect, something interesting is happening in Sweden.

The country has far more world-leading tech companies than it should in relation to its population. During this century, Stockholm has developed more billion-dollar tech companies, or 'unicorns', than any other city in Europe. Its successes include names such as Spotify (music on demand), Skype (internet telephony), iZettle (turning your cellphone into a cash register), Klarna (a sort of Scandi Mastercard with knobs on), Oatly (dairy-free milk), Mojang (makers of video game Minecraft) and King (who brought you Candy Crush

Saga and happily wasted many hours of your life). If you have played a game on your telephone today, listened to music online, or video-called a friend, the chances are that you used tech from a Swedish company.

As a result, Sweden's big cities have become some of the hottest locations for people seeking to create the next big thing in technology – green or otherwise. Paris, Rome and London might attract more tourists, but Stockholm is one of Europe's most active start-up hubs. How can this be? As we already know, Sweden has relatively high taxes and generous welfare programmes, a large public sector and an outlook on life that is ambivalent towards individual achievement. Yet the orthodox view holds that to encourage innovation, the state should keep out of the economy, cut taxes, slash budgets and tear up regulations, allowing entrepreneurs free rein to create new things. Sweden's record suggests, on the contrary, that there might be other ways of getting similar results.

Attempting to explain economic creativity feels foolhardy, given that so many subtle factors must combine before people can make remarkable stuff happen. There isn't anything as simple as a 'Swedish model' for innovation. On the other hand, it can't just be something in the water. In the second decade of the 21st century, several factors combined to put Sweden in a sweet spot for innovative enterprise. Some of these aspects are connected to the way that Swedish society is organised, but some are down to the alchemy of chance and human ingenuity, with the right individuals happening to be in the right place at the right time.

Let's look at society first. In 1982, my father purchased a ZX Spectrum, one of the first home computers, produced by a British company called Sinclair. He felt that his adolescent children should be exposed to the technology of the future. The seed fell on stony ground. We played digital ping-pong on the Spectrum a few times, and that was about it – a less tech-minded family it is hard to imagine. About 15 years later, however, Sweden went one better than my dad. Following an initiative from the big trade union federations, the government introduced subsidies to encourage people to buy personal computers. Within four years, around a million Swedes gained access to a PC. Doubtless, as was the case with my family, some of them were left to gather dust in an attic. But combined with the rollout of fast broadband across the country, this 'home PC reform' created a cohort of tech-savvy young people, just at a time when the economy required… a cohort of tech-savvy young people.

'It was not the intention to create entrepreneurs, but that was the result of the PC reform,' says Marie Wall, a start-up commissioner in Sweden's business ministry, whose job it is to coax more innovation out of the citizenry: 'You cannot innovate what you cannot imagine. So it was important to put technology into the hands of young people – playing games, learning to programme, getting their imagination going. It triggered them to go out and make change happen.' One of the people to make the most of the home PC revolution was Sebastian Siemiatkowski, co-founder of payments company Klarna: 'When I was young my family couldn't afford a computer. But because of this subsidy we could, and from the age of ten I was always playing around with it. [It] was very visionary of the politicians back then.'

In short, the state made its citizens more entrepreneurial, even if unintentionally. The same thing has happened in other ways. We have already touched on how the welfare system in Sweden can encourage people to take the risks involved in pursuing a business idea, by lessening the fear of failure and 'allowing people to dare' (see Chapter 8). But the public sector also subsidises entrepreneurship through the education system. University education in Sweden is free, although most students borrow from the state to cover their living expenses. More importantly, it is widely agreed that Swedish education encourages independent thinking and creativity.

'The general way that we raise kids is creative, we teach them to teach themselves,' says Mattias Hjelmstedt, Swedish co-founder of Utopia Music, a blockchain-powered music-tracking platform. After becoming one of the world's top computer gamers, Hjelmstedt has spent the 21st century creating tech companies while raising two children in London, New York, Los Angeles, Zurich and Barcelona. 'One thing you notice is that Swedes are a little different with their kids. We are not so much "You can't do this, you can't do that." The more rules you enforce, the less creative you are as a human being. And a lot of companies come out of being creative.'

Hjelmstedt's memories of school in Sweden in the 1980s and '90s are of being free to experiment – if something went wrong, it didn't matter. 'We don't force too much structure on our kids, which can be negative for creativity,' he says, a fact he thinks is often overlooked. The school system is 'broken' in most countries because it was designed for the industrial revolution and for building 'bricks in the wall, links in the chain'. Nowadays, Hjelmstedt believes, the job you wanted to educate yourself for at school no longer exists when you leave: 'You need a school system that teaches the fundamentals so you can then develop yourself. If you have a school system that doesn't embrace change you are educating people against where the world is heading.'

While creating the material conditions for an innovative culture, the Swedish state has encouraged entrepreneurship in more direct ways. Opening up the country to foreign competition in the 1990s meant a much bigger pool of investors interested in buying companies and making their owners rich – an incentive for starting your own business. The scrapping of wealth and inheritance taxes in the 2000s added more stimuli. Attitudes to entrepreneurship also changed. Being an entrepreneur used to be frowned upon. Even gambling was considered a more acceptable way to make your money than entrepreneurship, according to Jacob De Geer, co-founder of iZettle. 'If you made money from gambling or lottery that was okay,' he told a website. 'For most other things, making money and having money at that time wasn't really appropriate.'

High-profile successes encouraged others to go into business – the 'Björn Borg' model, Swedes call it. Just as the Swedish tennis star's international triumphs made tennis a much more popular sport at home, breakthroughs by new Swedish companies also created a buzz. 'Before, young people wanted to go into banks or Ericsson, but now they want to take a risk to realise their dreams by starting a company or going to work for a start-up,' serial Swedish entrepreneur Hjalmar Winbladh told *Forbes*. The Björn Borg effect came with an added twist in Sweden: thanks to relative equality of opportunity, if someone succeeds then everyone thinks they can do so too – a positive effect of the Jante Law (see Chapter 4). Wall says: 'There is a belief that there is no big difference between us, maybe because of the social security system, that there are no economic barriers to your kids, so everyone can make it'.

These are some of the social factors that have combined to create a start-up 'moment' in Sweden. To the list one could also add Sweden's unusually strong design ethos and early adopter culture, and its small domestic market that forces entrepreneurs to think globally from day one. A recent study found very high levels of 'intrapreneurship' among Swedish employees – almost three times the level in the United States – where workers are involved in innovative, entrepreneurial activity inside their existing employment. High levels of trust among Swedes relative to other countries makes collaboration easier in flexible environments that are more likely to spark new ideas, research suggests.

But key individuals have also played a role in making things happen.

During the first wave of Sweden's digital entrepreneurship in the 1990s, Marie Wall and her husband were active participants in Sweden's fledgling digital economy. Another central figure was Jan Stenbeck, a serial entrepreneur and leading figure at Kinnevik, a major Swedish investment company. In the early 1990s, Stenbeck had a 'fail-fast mentality' and risked his own money on young people with ideas. 'It was like another version of school,' Wall says. 'So many big players today started in that ecosystem.' Niklas Zennström, who went on to found Skype, was one of the figures to emerge from this environment of hectic experimentation.

But it was still too early. The dot-com bubble – when over-hyped hopes of digital riches ran into the reality of zero profits – wiped out a lot of these initiatives. The first wave of Sweden's start-up journey crashed at the start of the century.

However, Stenbeck's start-up 'school' had provided valuable experience to a new group of Swedish entrepreneurs. Their companies might have failed, but they themselves stuck around. As the market for digital products and services recovered, they were now better placed to respond. The success of companies such as Skype meant tech pioneers had money in their pockets and were looking for investment opportunities. More Swedes were now competent at scaling up tech companies, taking them from small-scale start-ups to enterprises with a global reach. The larger companies provided experience, networks, capital and customers for smaller ones, while the people who had invested in successful companies were now investing in new ones. Meanwhile, there was an ever-expanding talent pool of people looking to start their own companies. 'We had a critical mass,' Wall says. It had taken almost 25 years to build this start-up ecosystem, where smart minds could combine with the money and business acumen to turn ideas into companies.

Similar innovation ecosystems are at various stages of development all over Europe, and once they reach their own critical mass they will also take off. Sweden merely started out earlier, and in favourable circumstances – but there is nothing that guarantees that it will stay ahead of the start-up curve. In the meantime, the stars have aligned to make Sweden a fertile environment for people who want to turn ideas into stuff that can actually change the world.

Conclusion
The Future: What Can we Learn?

If you are ever fortunate to stay at a hotel in Sweden, look out for the breakfast buffet. Here you are likely to find a metal contraption with what looks like a bright blue toothpaste tube sticking out of it. When you turn the handle, it squeezes the tube, which squirts pale pink gunk onto your plate. This is Kalles Kaviar, a salt-sweet cod roe concoction that Swedes like to put on their eggs in the morning. It's a bit like Marmite – you either love it or loathe it. Sweden is like Kalles Kaviar. People tend to have strong opinions about it.

Others have compared the country to a Rorschach test – that thing that psychologists do when they make you look at an ink blot and tell them what you see. The picture you discern in the random pattern supposedly reflects your personality. In other words, whenever you talk about Sweden, you are going to superimpose your outlook on the facts. On the left, people seem to think Sweden is the country of milk and honey, a gentle, democratic socialism that takes from the rich and gives to the poor to make a decent society for all. Then there are conservatives who treat Sweden as a cautionary tale, not just because regulation and welfare supposedly destroy the work ethic and drag down the economy, but because an open, caring society will inevitably be overrun by Muslim immigrants, with heaven knows what disastrous consequences. 'What these groups see says more about them than about Sweden,' says Johan Norberg, maker of a 2018 documentary about Sweden.

Both these sets of views are exaggerated, both sides are misinformed – I have attempted to enlighten both right and left; no doubt it will annoy both sides. In any case, I think we can draw some firm and undisputed conclusions from what we have learned about this country.

First, there is a new Swedish model. It is not particularly new, in the sense that it emerged from the economic wreckage of the 1990s and so has been around for a while. But it is new in the sense that most people's opinions of it need updating. Also, the past two decades have served to demonstrate a basic characteristic of it: it is a shared creature of both left and right, created by political consensus. It is no longer true to say that the Swedish model is social democratic – keen-eyed business people and the conservative centre-right are happy to espouse its key features.

The new Swedish model is not the same as the 1970s version. Sweden has accepted fiscal discipline – a low inflation target, balanced budgets, limited deficits – partly imposed by membership of the EU, and partly a response to the perceived profligacy of the 1980s. The central bank has been independent of government since 1999. Large chunks of the public sector are now in private hands. Foreign companies can purchase Swedish businesses, even the big ones. Wealth and inheritance taxes have been scrapped, and rates of taxation are nothing out of the ordinary.

Swedish attitudes have changed, too. When asked what the Swedish model stood for in 2012, Swedes put tax-funded schools and welfare in first place, unsurprisingly – generous welfare is quintessentially Swedish. More unexpected was the answer that came in second place: 'Everyone has the right to choose schools and healthcare centres.' These sorts of choices were nowhere to be seen 40 years ago.

An important aspect of the new Swedish model is a continuation from the past – centralised wage bargaining, where the international competitiveness of Sweden's main export industries sets the benchmark for all sectors. This in turn keeps the wage structure relatively flat and high, forcing industry to innovate or die. This aspect of the old 1960s model fell apart in the 1980s but was resurrected in the late '90s. In turn, it depends upon a tradition of mutual trust forged in the 1930s, in which trade unions acquiesce in the need for constant upheaval and change, while employers take some responsibility for the consequences of restructuring for workers.

Another feature of the model is the apparent dominance of investors with a long-term view of business, hardwired into their outlook through the system of dual shares. Corporate power lies not with management but with shareholders who are

obliged to take part in big, strategic decisions. Instead of anony-
mous investment funds or small investors focused on making a
quick buck, there are strong owners with a name, a responsibility
and a clear role. This approach is combined with a management
style that emphasises consensus and involvement. It may be
cumbersome at times, but it gives momentum to business decisions, and encourages initiative. These factors have helped a
small country create some of the biggest names in global industry.
In the second decade of the millennium, they also combined to
create a very creative entrepreneurial environment.

The model has made it a priority to help women combine
work with having a family. To weaken the tendency for women
to take on a double burden of domestic and professional work,
it has used carrots and sticks to encourage men to share the
burden of childcare. Starting in the 1960s from a need to fill a
gaping hole in the workforce, Swedish family policy was also
driven by the notion that sex discrimination is economically
inefficient. Today it has acquired a further justification, with
governments of left and right espousing feminism as part of
a wider ambition to be a beacon for humanitarianism and
human rights.

This has also fostered an openness to asylum and immigration, though this is being tested by the most recent influx of
refugees from various man-made catastrophes. The model has
gained a reputation for being environmentally conscious, and
aspects of Swedish capitalism would appear to lend themselves
to the vision, ambition and organisation necessary to effect a
green transformation of industry and society. But it is too early

to say whether the country's latest mission to become carbon neutral by 2045 is more than a green gloss on a problem that requires more fundamental change.

The term 'model' is a retrospective construction, and there is a tendency to see it as an empty bottle into which you can pour any wine of your choice; far from being fixed, you can project whatever you want onto it. According to this view, the Swedish model is little more than good branding. Based on the evidence gathered here, I would beg to differ. Yes, the Swedish model is undoubtedly a good brand name and, yes, here are different interpretations of what is fundamental to it. But there is something more substantial here, aspects of an economy that are real and effable and distinct. The fact that important features of the model fell apart in the 1980s and were pieced back together again helps us to see their significance in sharper outline today.

As an economy, Sweden looks much more like the rest of the world today than it did back then. And yet it is different. If it wasn't different, it wouldn't provoke such passionate views for and against. Moreover, this model has been championed in Sweden by both centre-left and centre-right governments during the past two decades – there is plenty of room for debate over emphasis and direction, but there is agreement over the underlying parameters.

So what can we learn from it? Here comes the Rorschach test.

Sweden is living proof that regulated capitalism can generate effective and sustainable economic growth, and that the state can play a useful role. This is a society that, on the one hand, adheres to the principles of a market economy, includ-ing competition, free trade, openness and innovation. On the other, it does not suffer from a naive belief that markets are self-regulatory and that politics should be all about dereg-ulation, tax cuts and paring back the state. It is based on an understanding that, in order to create human welfare as well as growth, the market economy needs an extensive public system of regulation.

The Swedish experience suggests that workplace hierar-chies can be damaging to a modern business, and that to be productive, people need to feel they have a voice. Democracy in Western societies too often ends at the office entrance or the factory gate. How much endless energy is wasted on maintaining workplace hierarchies? How much creative potential is thrown away by crushing employees' motivation and initiative? Industrial democracy is an essential part of a modern economy. Trade unions are part of the solution, not the problem.

Restructuring, crisis, creative destruction – these are integral parts of capitalist enterprise. Unemployment is too often seen by governments as a policy tool for controlling wages, rather than a blight on society and a criminal waste of human potential. Sweden has hit on a means of dealing with layoffs in a more sensible, humane and far-sighted way through its transition system. This is a joint creation of unions and employers, based on the cast-iron certainty that things can get worse as well as better, so let's prepare for when they get worse. How much effort is wasted fighting to keep jobs because losing them will be a catastrophe for the employees concerned? How much time, money and motivation is wasted getting rid of employees, when a cyclical upturn in a year or two will see the business short of staff? Sweden's solution deserves international attention.

This leads to another lesson – it pays not be obsessed with short-term personal interest in business. The entire history of capitalism tells us this, and yet still the world walked into the financial crash of 2008, causing untold misery to millions, because the instruments used by its main financial institutions were all about short-term greed rather than long-term need. I don't think Sweden has found a solution to this. Levels of household debt are much too high, and the housing market has bubble-like features. But anything that encourages long-term thinking, such as Sweden's business ownership structure, deserves to be studied.

Why do governments make it so hard for families with children? The economics of childcare needs to change radically in Britain and the United States, at the very least. It is hypocrisy for politicians to claim to put families first and complain about our ageing society, at the same time as doing nothing about the realities of working life that make it so hard to have children. Without accessible and affordable childcare, it is women whose pay and careers suffer when they start a family. Sweden is not a gender-equal society. But it recognises that childcare is essential to achieving equality, as well as making good economic sense by allowing women to combine careers with having families.

Sweden has gone from being a monocultural society to one of the most multicultural in the world, in the space of a few decades. Has this been a disaster for Sweden? Categorically, no. Has it all been plain sailing? Absolutely not. Is recent human history characterised by large migrations? Are developed countries short of workers? Does it make any sense for the richest countries to accept the smallest numbers of migrants, when poor countries accept them as a matter of course? Is it hypocrisy for rich countries to turn away migrants fleeing the consequences of rich-nation policies? Sweden has at least woken up to these questions. In 2015, when there was humanitarian disaster in the Middle East, it opened its doors to tens of thousands of desperate people. It then slammed them shut again, because other EU countries refused to respond in the same way. It is now integrating these refugees into its society, with varying degrees of success. If we want to see the future of immigration in developed nations, then we need to look at Sweden, warts and all.

Some of Sweden's distinct features come together when we talk about the environment. A history of taking bold political initiatives, a consensus culture, a long-term outlook and suspicion of short-termism, centrally planned housing construction, municipal intervention, and partnerships with the private sector have all combined to create conditions in which Sweden could commit to going carbon neutral by 2045, and have a chance of actually doing so.

First, partnerships between the public and private sectors are helpful when large and risky investments need to be made, such as carbon capture and storage technologies. 'If we want that to happen, government has to team up with industry – it will cost taxpayers' money at the beginning,' says Oskar Larsson of the climate department at the Swedish Environmental Protection Agency. Larsson also points to a collaboration between a private Swedish steel company, a publicly owned iron ore miner and a public utility, backed by the state, to develop a zero-emissions method for making steel. Called Hybrit, this project – if successful – could revolutionise steel production worldwide and slash Sweden's total carbon emissions by 10 per cent.

Stockholm city maintains a 50 per cent stake in the heating side of Fortum, the private business that co-runs heating and power generation in the city. This is an important factor in Stockholm's goal to become carbon-free by 2040, five years before the rest of the country, says Björn Hugosson, Stockholm's climate boss. 'The lesson is that if you have a system you control, you can take measures to phase out emissions,' he says. 'When power stations are in the hands of private owners, you can't.'

Second, a green transformation of the economy will create losers – companies, industries and even entire sectors will have to be closed down. How you deal with so-called 'stranded assets' like this is an issue that climate policymakers have not dealt with very well, according to Anders Wijkman, the climate guru we met earlier. Sweden's transition system makes the country better equipped than most to cope with closing down parts of the economy that are an obstacle to achieving climate objectives.

CONCLUSION

So what of the future for the new Swedish model? This is modern welfare capitalism, and – for now, at least – it is functioning relatively well according to standard measures of success for capitalist economies. Emmanuel Macron, the current French president, who has proposed a 'third way' between right and left, has made much of the Nordic model as providing solutions for France. The impeccably free-market *Economist* magazine has proclaimed that the Nordics, Sweden included, are 'the next supermodel' countries that have 'reached the future first' and are offering 'highly innovative solutions that reject the tired orthodoxies of left and right'. Natalia Brzezinski, chief executive of Brilliant Minds, an annual tech conference in Stockholm, says: 'People are talking about the Swedish model now, they are realising there is something special to be proud of, but it has all been hidden. The tech people have done a lot, they have made Swedes proud. This country is a symbol of what can be done, there should be a coming-out party for the Swedish model – it has been a sleepy place for so long.'

There is much, much more to the Swedish model than some sort of doe-eyed multiculturalism and handouts for the work-shy. However, some might see a threat to the model from the rapid rise of the far-right Sweden Democrats, who have become a vocal opposition to immigration. Certainly their arrival in or close to government would deliver a blow to Sweden's image abroad. Unlike other right-wing populist parties in Scandinavia, the Sweden Democrats have their roots in the neo-Nazis, and despite efforts to rid the party of

258

its more radical elements, high votes for the party go hand in hand with outbursts of grass-roots racism. But as far as image is concerned, Sweden may not have so much to fear. Denmark, which long ago jettisoned any pretence of social liberalism, still enjoys a cuddly image abroad associated with *hygge* – the Danish art of cosiness – when it is so clearly *hygge* for some and not for others. In Norway and Finland far-right parties have recently enjoyed ministerial positions, while in Denmark their support kept a minority centre-right administration in power. There is nothing exceptional about Sweden that would prevent its politics from going in similar directions.

The inroads made by far-right populists are a sign that all is not well with the country. Significant numbers of people feel left out. This book presents a top-down view of Swedish society, from people for whom life is comfortable and the model is working fine. Looked at from below, most Swedes lead busy, hard-working lives holding down jobs and raising families; margins are tight, and some find it more of a struggle than others. If the economy fails to deliver for them, then they will look for alternatives on the left and the right. But the Swedish model is about much more than politics. Further successes for populists would challenge the fundamentals, but not erase them – the underlying features of the model are likely to be around for a while to come.

Sweden's high dependence on the world economy makes it vulnerable to the vagaries of capitalism beyond its borders. But it came through the 2008 crash better than most, and has built buffers against future crises. In Soviet times, Russians used to joke: why is Western capitalism on the edge of a precipice? Answer: So they can get a better look at us down here. That rather sums up Sweden's position relative to a systemic crisis. This society has problems like any other, but for those at the top looking down – it doesn't feel that the problems are likely to bring them crashing down any time soon. The challenge, in the meantime, is to make the model work better for more people.

Acknowledgements

Many people have given their time to help create this book, not least those who agreed to be interviewed and the people who arranged those interviews. The Karl-Adam Bonnier Foundation in Stockholm commissioned the research for an earlier version of this book – published in 2018 as *Bumblebee Nation: The Hidden Story of the New Swedish Model* – and gave me freedom to follow my own nose. How I carried out this project is entirely my own responsibility. Mats Bergstrand shared his connections. Beth Eynon at Blink made a brilliant edit. Thanks also to Heather Farmbrough, Eric Zsiga, Peter Jervelycke Belfrage, Camilla and Steve Flood, and Orla Vigsø for editorial insight and painstaking corrections, and to Karin Wallström Nordén for allowing me flexibility to fit this project around my other work commitments. Thank you to my wonderful family and friends in England for helping me through the big leap north. Annika introduced me to a new life in Sweden, for which my gratitude is boundless.

Sources

All the quotes in this book are from interviews with the author, unless otherwise stated in the text or below. The author conducted more than 70 interviews in Sweden between December 2016 and May 2018.

Introduction: Famous for six hours

My *Guardian* article that seems to have started all the rumours: David Crouch, 'Efficiency up, turnover down: Sweden experiments with six-hour working day', theguardian.com, 17 September 2015

That *Herald* quote: 'Robert McNeil on... Swedish six-hour working day', www.heraldscotland.com, 21 September 2015

That viral Facebook video: www.facebook.com/enjoy.science/ videos/329209404093610/

Chapter 1: Almost different

Average vodka consumption reached almost a litre a week for every man, woman and child... Richard F. Tomasson, 'Alcohol and alcohol control in Sweden', *Scandinavian Studies*, Vol. 70, No. 4, 1998, pp.477–508

In 2018, a staggering 77 per cent of Sweden were in favour of the state alcohol monopoly... The stats are published in Systembolaget's annual reports

Systembolaget is the most trusted institution in Sweden... This is from *Förtroendebarometern* 2019, issued each year by Medieakademin

High marginal tax rates on the rich... See, for example: the useful charts in Andreas Bergh, *Sweden and the Revival of the Capitalist Welfare State*, Edward Elgar Publishing, 2016

The numbers employed by the public sector are contained in D. Johansson, 'The Number and the Size Distribution of Firms in Sweden and Other European Countries', IUI Working Papers 483, Stockholm: Industriens Utredningsinstitut, 1997, and in *Government At A Glance* 2017, by the OECD, Paris, 2017

Sweden beats other countries at just about everything... Alex Gray, 'Sweden beats other countries at just about everything', www.weforum.org, 30 January 2017

When you take out the long holidays that Swedes enjoy, their productivity compares well to that of the United States... Paul Krugman, 'The truth about the Nordic economies', www.nytimes.com, 27 October 2018

Chapter 2: Unions

That survey of hair colour is in H. Lundborg, *The Racial Characters of the Swedish Nation*, Anthropologia Suecica 1926, published by Forgotten Books, 2018

Frantzén quote: Johan Ronge, 'Fackets hårda krav mot Sveriges rikaste kvinna', expressen.se, 22 February 2018

The bumblebee quote by Göran Persson is taken from his opening address to a conference of Sweden's Social Democratic Party in Stockholm on 10 March 2000, and is quoted in Subhash

Thakur *et al.*, *Sweden's Welfare State: Can the Bumblebee Keep Flying?*, International Monetary Fund, Washington D.C., 2003

For a good summary of the early decades of Swedish labour relations, see Anders Kjellberg, 'The Swedish Model of Industrial Relations: Self-Regulation and Combined Centralisation-Decentralisation', in Craig Phelan (ed.), *Trade Unionism since 1945: Towards a Global History*, Vol. 1, 2009, pp.155–198

Bedrock of the Swedish model: Richard Milne, 'Global threat fails to break spirit of Sweden's labour model', FT.com, 6 January 2014

Since 1991, the wages of the average LO member have gone up a remarkable 60 per cent in real terms... See the OECD's data on average wages here: https://data.oecd.org/earnwage/average-wages.htm

Average wages in Sweden have indeed risen smoothly and steadily over the past three decades... As above. Ireland's average wages have risen by more, but they also came down sharply after the country's financial crisis

TCO video about Joe Williams, by PR Bureau ANR BBDO: vimeo.com/84733222

TCO 'Business like a Swede' video, also by PR Bureau ANR BBDO: www.youtube.com/watch?v=OcVoKPTS7AU

The second most shared video on YouTube in its first 24 hours... Angelica Rylin, 'Storytelling – Like a Swede', angelicarylin.wordpress.com, 13 October 2014

Chapter 3: Management

Labour Policy Council survey of business attitudes to the unions: Hur Fungerar Kollektivavtalen? Arbetsmarknadsekonomiska rådet, Stockholm, 2018

Chapter 4: The future is flat

'A flat corporate structure is a logical and cost-efficient way to operate...' Pär Isaksson, *Leading Companies in a Global Age – Managing the Swedish Way*, Stockholm, VINNOVA Swedish Governmental Agency for Innovation Systems, 2008

For more on the Swedish management style, see: C. Bjursell, 'Transformative leadership: A Swedish case', in: Daphne Halkias, Joseph C. Santora, Nicholas Harkiolakis, Paul W. Thurman (eds), *Leadership and Change Management: A Cross-Cultural Perspective*, Routledge, 2017, pp.114-119; Fredrik Movitz and Åke Sandberg, *All Gone but Still There: The Swedish Model and Swedish Management. On Scandinavian Perspectives on Management in Swedish Working Life*, Department of Sociology, University of Stockholm, 2011; Tor Grenness, 'Will the 'Scandinavian leadership model' survive the forces of globalisation? A SWOT analysis', *International Journal of Business and Globalisation* 7(3), 2011, 332–350; I. Holmberg and S. Åkerblom, 'Primus Inter Pares – Leadership and Culture in Sweden', in J. S. Chokar *et al.* (eds) *Culture and Leadership Across the World: The GLOBE Book of In-Depth Studies of 25 Societies*. New Jersey, Lawrence Erlbaum Associates, 2007; Bengt Gustavsson, 'Human values in Swedish management', *Journal of Human Values*, 1, 1995, 153–71

Ginny Figlar's quote is taken from her article 'Swedishness has no borders', highlights.ikea.com, 2016

Chapter 5: Pain

To protect her privacy, Gunilla Stensson is not her real name, but she is a very real person

When I was researching this book, I began to feel that I had made a genuine discovery in revealing the hidden welfare system in Sweden that helps people change jobs. So little had been written about it elsewhere, even in Swedish. But then Alana Semuels, a staff writer for the *Atlantic* magazine in New York, wrote a brilliant piece about Sweden's job security agencies, asking: 'What If Getting Laid Off Wasn't Something to Be Afraid Of?' theatlantic.com, 25 October 2017. *The New York Times* did an interesting 'follow' a couple of months later: Peter S. Goodman, 'The Robots Are Coming, and Sweden Is Fine', NYTimes.com, 27 December 2017. The OECD issued a report on the system in 2015, entitled *Back to Work: Sweden – Improving the Re-employment Prospects of Displaced Workers.*

Chapter 6: Transition

As Meidner himself put it many years later... Meidner quoted by Mark Blyth, 'The transformation of the Swedish model', World Politics, 54, October 2001, pp.1–26. (The original quote is from a book dated 1984, which I have not read.)

LO's attitude to globalisation and structural transformation as 'opportunities rather than threats': Thomas Carlén, *Inequality is Bad for Business – A Progressive Agenda for Equality*, LO, Report to the World Economic Forum, Davos, 2017

86 per cent of Swedes agree with the statement that 'globalisation is an opportunity for economic growth': Eurobarometer, 'Designing Europe's Future: Trust in Institutions, Globalisation, Support for the Euro, Opinions About Free Trade and Solidarity', Special Eurobarometer 461, European Union, 2017

A remarkably flat society in terms of earned income... That and the following paragraph are based on Douglas A. Hibbs Jr. and Håkan Locking, 'Wage Dispersion and Productive Efficiency: Evidence for Sweden', *Journal of Labor Economics* 18, No. 4 (October 2000): 755–782

Elvander: it ended the confrontation regime... Nils Elvander, 'Industriavtalet och Saltsjöbadsavtalet – en jämförelse', Arbets-marknad & Arbetsliv 8 (3), 2002, pp.191–204

Chapter 7: Conflict

'Full-blown confrontation regime...' Nils Elvander, as above

Public debt doubled... Pär Nuder, *Saving the Swedish Model*, Institute for Public Policy Research, London, 2012

Meidner's remark that 'The Swedish system, balancing private ownership and social control, has broken down.' Rudolph Meidner, 'Why Did the Swedish Model Fail?' Socialist Register, 1993, 211–228

The original text of the Industry Agreement is also available in English: 'Agreement on industrial development and wage formation', Almega, 1997, and can be found here: www.indus-triradet.se

The economic history sections of this chapter also draw on the following sources: Interview with Per Ewaldsson, senior legal advisor, Medlingsinstitutet; Kristina Ahlen, 'Swedish Collective Bargaining Under Pressure', *British Journal of Industrial Relations*, 27:3, November 1989, pp.330–346; Dominique Anxo and Harald Niklasson, *The Swedish Model: Revival After the Turbulent 1990s?*, ILO Discussion Paper, 200; Andreas Bergh, 'On the Rise, Fall and Revival of a Capitalist Welfare State', *New Political Economy*, Vol. 19, Issue 5, 2014, pp.662–694; Thomas Carlén, 'Adapting the Nordic Model', in David Coates (ed.), *Exiting from the Crisis*, 2011, pp.189–195; Lennart Erixon, 'The Rehn-Meidner Model in Sweden: Its Rise, Challenges and Survival', *Journal of Economic Issues*, Vol. 44, Issue 3, 2010, pp.677–715; Lennart Erixon, 'The Rehn–Meidner model's relation to contemporary economics and the Stockholm School', *The European Journal of the History of Economic Thought*, Vol. 18, 2011, Issue 1, pp.85–123; Johannes Lindvall, 'Vad hände med den aktiva arbets-marknadspolitiken?', *Ekonomisk Debatt*, Vol. 39, No. 3, 2011, pp.38–45; Juhana Vartiainen, *To Create and Share – The Remarkable Success and Contested Future of the Nordic Social-Democratic Model*, FAFO, 2014; Juhana Vartiainen, 'Nordic Collective Agreements', in Lars Mjøset (ed.), *The Nordic Varieties of Capitalism*, 2015, pp.331–363; Ilya Viktorov, 'The Swedish Employers and the Wage-Earner Funds Debate during the Crisis of Fordism in the 1970s and 1980s', Conference Paper, Stockholm University, Department of Economic History, 2009

Chapter 8: Belief

Lars Walter's book on the job security agencies is Walter (ed.), *Mellan jobb. Omställningsavtal och stöd till uppsagda i Sverige*, Stockholm, SNS Förlag, 2015

The quote from Niklas Adalberth is taken from a 2015 interview I did with him for the *Financial Times*: David Crouch, 'Klarna: payments company lets customers try before they pay', FT.com, 5 June 2015

Silicon valley seems oblivious to the value of experience... Hannah Kuchler, 'No country for middle-aged techies', FT.com, 28 April 2017

The OECD stats on Swedish skill levels are in *Skills Outlook 2017: Skills and Global Value Chains*, OECD, 2017

Chapter 9: Jungle capitalism

Canadian scepticism about Haparanda: Minutes of the Standing Committee on Foreign Affairs and International Development, House of Commons, Canada, 20 November 2012

Some general background to the Haparanda IKEA deal: David
Carr, 'Det hemliga spelet om Ikea', nsd.se, 27 September 2016

Kamprad's 'jungle capitalism' quote: 'Ingvar Kamprad ser en ny
sorts marknadsekonomi', svd.se, 12 December 2005

'We fell in love…' Torkel Omnell, 'Dokument: Buchts kamp för
Ikea', nsd.se, 15 November 2006

On the 'Anglo-Saxon model', see the succinct definition given
by Gideon Rachman, chief foreign affairs columnist at the
Financial Times: 'Definition of Anglo-Saxon capitalism',
lexicon.ft.com (no date)

Chapter 10: The 100-year plan

Richard Twomey, 'Sweden, you have got to be joking…' Quoted by
Richard Milne, 'Meet the Wallenbergs', FT.com, 15 June 2015

On dual shares, Facebook and Google: Andrea Tan and Benjamin
Robertson, 'Why Investors Are Fretting Over Dual-Class Shares',
bloomberg.com, 10 July 2017

On dual shares in Sweden, see for example: 'Our company right or
wrong', economist.com, 15 March 2007

Fredrik Lundberg's rare interview with the *Financial Times*:
Richard Milne, 'Sweden's new business king takes the long-
term view', FT.com, 5 January 2015. Lundberg declined to be
interviewed for this book

The Swedish economy is increasingly owned from abroad: foreign
ownership on the Stockholm stock exchange rose from 8 per
cent in 1991 to 41 per cent in 2017. Of what is left, 15 Swedish
families control 70 per cent. In 2017, the 15 largest business
families managed companies worth £410 billion (by comparison, Sweden's total economic output in the same year was
£380 billion). The Wallenberg family controls companies
valued at almost £16 billion. See Majsa Allelin *et al.* (2018),

'Ägande- och förmögenhetsstrukturen och dess förändring sedan 1980', Katalys 55, 3–35

Chapter 12: The limits of *lagom*

Sweden loses more than £3.4 billion in tax revenue each year... See, for example: 'Jätteläcka visar hur rika undviker skatt,' sveriges-radio.se, 5 November 2017

'This is not how it works in Sweden...' Quoted by Pär Karlsson, 'M-ledaren sågar Östling för skatteuttalande', aftronbladet.se, 7 November 2017

'Royalty that celebrates its privileges...' PM Nilsson, 'De rika och legitimiteten', di.se, 26 January 2015. I took a brief look at Swedish attitudes to the monarchy for *The Guardian*: David Crouch, 'Sweden gears up for royal wedding as republican sentiments rise,' theguardian.com, 12 June 2015

Quotes from experts on inequality in Sweden are taken from research I did for a *Guardian* article: David Crouch, 'The new "people's home": how Sweden is waging war on inequality', theguardian.com, 17 July 2017. Some quotes are from the article itself

The source of Per Molander's remark about the rapid increase of inequality in Sweden can be found in OECD documents, such as 'OECD Income inequality data update: Sweden (January 2015)', which states that the growth in inequality in Sweden between 1985 and the early 2010s was the largest among all OECD countries, increasing by one -third.

Angel Gurría is quoted in 'Inequality hurts economic growth, finds OECD research', oecd.org, 9 December 2014

On the IMF, see for example: Prakash Loungani and Jonathan D. Ostry, 'The IMF's Work on Inequality: Bridging Research and Reality', blogs.imf.org, 22 February 2017; Angela Gaviria, 'Response to Article: "The IMF is Showing Some Hypocrisy on Inequality"', imf.org, 16 February 2017

Chapter 13: Freedom

That internet forum discussing the situation for Swedish women abroad: http://www.familjeliv.se/forum/thread/57154370-barnomsorg-utomlands

Chapter 14: Equality

'In order that women shall be emancipated from their antiquated role...' Olof Palme, 'The Emancipation of Man', address to the Women's National Democratic Club, Washington D.C., 8 June 1970

'We have to expand society's facilities for childcare...' Olof Palme, speech at the UN Conference of International Women's Year, Mexico City, 23 June 1975

In the 1950s, Sweden had a lower participation rate of women in the workforce than Britain... Mary Ruggie, *The State and Working Women: A Comparative Study of Britain and Sweden*, Princeton University Press, 1984, p.144

The number of publicly provided childcare spaces increased rapidly... Kimberly Earles, 'Swedish Family Policy – Continuity and Change in the Nordic Welfare State', *Social Policy & Administration*, Vol. 45, No. 2, 2011, pp.180–193

Simultaneously, the amount of paid time off for parents... Ann-Zofie Duvander, 'Svensk föräldraförsäkrings utveckling och konsekvenser', *Søkelys på arbeidslivet*, Vol. 34, No. 01–02, 2017, pp.126–143

The number of fathers taking paternity leave had stalled... Katrin Bennhold, 'In Sweden, Men Can Have It All,' NYTimes.com, 9 June 2010

'The lack of gender equality is not only an injustice...' Bengt Westerberg and others, 'Ökad jämställdhet: Motion till riksdagen 1985/86:A604', 27 January 1986

'I always thought if we made it easier for women to work...'
Westerberg interviewed by Bennhold, see above

Subsidised childcare places expanded to nearly 730,000 by 2002.
The figure is cited by Earles, see above

Fathers take around a quarter of the total parental leave on average...
Duvander, see above

Sweden spends four times as much of its wealth on early childhood
education and care than the United States... Claudia Olivetti and
Barbara Petrongolo, 'The Economic Consequences of Family
Policies: Lessons from a Century of Legislation in High-Income
Countries', *Journal of Economic Perspectives*, Vol. 31, No. 1,
2017, pp.205–230

Despite the economic crisis of the early 1990s, Sweden still managed
to expand its system of childcare... Sweden is not alone in this
respect. A study by the OECD found that, in an era of perceived
permanent austerity and overall welfare state retrenchment,
rich countries have not been prevented from expanding family
policies. Emanuele Ferragina and Martin Seeleib-Kaiser,
'Determinants of a Silent (R)evolution: Understanding the
Expansion of Family Policy in Rich OECD Countries', *Social
Politics*, Vol. 22, No. 1, 2014, pp.1–37

On the Sweden Democrats and women's equality, see Diana Mulinari
Anders Neergaard, 'Doing Racism, Performing Femininity:
Women in the Sweden Democrats', in Michaela Köttig *et al.*
(eds), *Gender and Far Right Politics in Europe*, e-book, Palgrave,
2017, pp.13–27

Chapter 15: #MeToo

Hwang and Haas reported a dramatic increase in corporate support
in large Swedish companies for fathers taking leave... Linda
Haas and C. Philip Hwang, 'Is Fatherhood Becoming More

Visible at Work? Trends in Corporate Support for Fathers Taking Parental Leave in Sweden', *Fathering*, Vol. 7, No. 3, 2009, pp.303–321

'The male norm of full-time employment remains strong...' C. Philip Hwang, 'Even when fathers take lots of parental leave, mothers end up with more responsibility for childcare. Why?', https://fatherhood.global, 31 May 2016

Swedish women experience a large drop in relative earnings... See, for example, Nikolay Angelov *et al.*, 'Parenthood and the Gender Gap in Pay', *Journal of Labor Economics*, Vol. 34, No. 3, 2016, pp.545–579; James Albrecht *et al.*, 'Parental Leave and the Glass Ceiling in Sweden', presentation at the European Society of Population Economics in Braga, Portugal, June 2014

Chapter 16: The People's Home

On Koppargården, see Josefine Hökerberg's award-winning reports for Dagens Nyheter, including 'Kissblöjorna vägs – för att spara pengar', dn.se, 11 November 2011, and 'Carema försökte köpa min tystnad när pappa dog', dn.se, 12 October 2011

Swedes opposed to companies making profits at all in the welfare sector... Lennart Nilsson, *Välfärdspolitik och välfärdsopinion 1986–2012 Vinster i välfärden?*, som.gu.se, n.d.

On the changes in Swedish elderly care, see for example: Gabrielle Meagher and Marta Szebehely (eds), *Marketisation in Nordic Eldercare: A Research Report on Legislation, Oversight, Extent and Consequences*, Stockholm Studies in Social Work 30, 2013

On the problems of Sweden's free schools, see Helen Warrell, 'Free schools: Lessons in store', ft.com, 27 August 2014, and David Crouch, 'OECD urges Sweden to reform schools system', ft.com, 4 May 2015

For insider criticism of the pension reforms, see for example: Jan Hagberg and Ellis Wohlner, 'The Market for Social Insecurity:

A shady pension reform entices economic elites and clouds the future of Sweden's elderly', *Scandinavian Insurance Quarterly* 4, 2002, 333–340

The number of hospital beds has fallen to the lowest per capita in the developed world... Catherine Edwards, 'Why family-friendly Sweden is talking about a maternity care crisis', the local.se, 24 January 2018

Carema boss's salary: Ida Yttergren, 'Ett vinsttak tar död på hela branschen', dn.se, 2 February 2018

On Jan Emanuel Johansson see, for example: Michael Syrén, 'Ny supervinst för Jan Emanuel – på flyktingar', expressen.se, 15 August 2017

That former anti-immigrant politician making money from immigrants:.David Crouch, 'Former Swedish rightwing populist is saviour of Syrian refugees', ft.com, 29 December 2013

On the benefits of weighing diapers see, for example: L. Hellström, N. Zubotikin, P. Ekelund, M.E. Larsson, I. Milsom, 'Selecting the correct incontinence pad in nursing home patients by pad weighing'. Arch Gerontol Geriatr. Mar–Apr 1994; 18(2):125–32

Chapter 17: Riot

'Maybe I should change his name...' The quote is from Martin Sandbu and David Crouch, 'Riots in Sweden: Fire in the people's home', FT.com, 24 May 2013. On grievances against racism and the police, see David Couch, 'Stockholm violence exposes grievances against the police', FT.com, 23 May 2013

'Spending more of the nation's income on foreign aid than any other country in 2015...' According to the OECD's statistics here: https://data.oecd.org/oda/net-oda.htm

Reinfeldt's 'open your hearts' speech was widely reported. His remarks about Sweden having 'more space than you can imagine' are less well known. They are quoted by Hanna Jakobson, 'Fredrik Reinfeldt: Gott om plats för flyktingar', expressen.se, 7 December 2014

'My Europe doesn't build walls...' Tal av statsminister Stefan Löfven vid manifestationen för flyktingar, Medborgarplatsen, Stockholm, den 6 september 2015, regeringen.se

'It pains me that Sweden is no longer capable of receiving asylum seekers...' Quoted in David Crouch, 'Sweden slams shut its open-door policy towards refugees', theguardian.com, 24 November 2015

The country was set up as a whipping boy for multiculturalism... In the first six months of 2017, far-right website Breitbart published well over 100 articles claiming that immigration was wreaking havoc in Sweden (Paul Rapacioli, *Good Sweden, Bad Sweden: The Use and Abuse of Swedish Values in a Post Truth World*, Stockholm, Volante, 2018, p.56). Britain's *Daily Mail* was not far behind in conducting an orchestrated campaign against Sweden's asylum policy. The racist message was relentless – 'black people are violent criminals'. At the time of writing (May 2018), this crude message continues to be pumped out from an unholy alliance of Alt Right websites and Kremlinbacked organisations such as Russia Today and Sputnik

Chapter 18: Jobs

Minimum wages in Sweden were twice as high as in most developed countries... These IMF statistics were sent to me by SEB

More than half of the total unemployed would consist of people born outside the country... In the final quarter of 2016, 335,000 people were unemployed in Sweden, of whom 160,000 – or 48 per cent – were foreign born. Arbetsmarknadssituationen för hela befolkningen 15–74 år, AKU Fjärde kvartalet 2016, scb.se, 14 February 2017

Employment rates among low-skilled immigrants were far lower than those of native Swedes... *Finding the Way: A Discussion of the Swedish Migrant Integration System*, OECD, Paris, 2014

Seven years or more on average for a new arrival to get work... A 2015 report for the Swedish government found that it took between seven and ten years for just 50 per cent of new arrivals to find a job. *Nyanländas etablering – är statens insatser effektiva?* RiR 2015:17, Riksrevisionen, Stockholm, 2017

Stefan Löfven, 'Sweden is at a crossroads...' Speech in Stockholm on 29 February 2016: 'Striden om den svenska modellen', socialdemokraterna.se

'A grenade under the Swedish model'... Olof Svensson, 'Kritiken: Annie Lööf driver en Sovjetpolitik', aftonbladet.se, 5 February 2016

'The typical Swedish way of solving problems is the pragmatic way...' The agreement on subsidised etableringsjobb was announced in March 2018

Chapter 19: Homes

Ek and Lorentzon's open letter: 'Vi måste agera eller bli omsprungna!' medium.com/@SpotifySE, 12 April 2016

'It is almost impossible for immigrants and new arrivals to penetrate this market...' Quoted in David Crouch, 'Pitfalls of rent restraints: why Stockholm's model has failed many', theguardian.com, 19 August 2015

The Housing Board's bombshell estimate: 'Reviderad prognos över behovet av nya bostäder till 2025', boverket.se, June 2016

According to the Tenants Union... Lee Roden, 'The story of Sweden's housing crisis', thelocal.se, 28 August 2017

Getting to the front of the line in central Stockholm takes 20 years... 'Almost 580,000 now waiting for apartments in Stockholm', thelocal.se, 16 August 2017

Property prices rose six-fold in 20 years... See the chart provided by Eshe Nelson, 'Sweden's cooling housing market is a preview for others with low rates and property bubbles', qz.com, 25 November, 2017. The average debt-to-income ratio for households with mortgages was 338 per cent in September 2016, according to Sweden's central bank, while total household debt was 86 per cent of GDP

'Historic' investment in more housing: 'Stöd som ska gynna ökat bostadsbyggande', regering.se, 24 March 2017

'Let me put it this way...' Henrik Landelius quoted in 'Sweden's housing shortage from a builder's perspective', sverigesradio.se, 25 February 2016

The forecast for 2018 was for a dip in construction... 'Bostadsbyggandet kan nå en topp i år', boverket.se, 9 November 2017

In one school just two of its 750 pupils are classified as ethnic Swedish... Richard Milne, 'Sweden immigration: Don't look back', FT.com, 5 October 2015

Chapter 20: Souls on fire

Groups like this were initially praised by politicians... I am thinking here primarily of Hammenhög in southern Sweden, which was praised by the Migration Board and Conservative migration minister Tobias Billström in 2013 as a model for Sweden

And there, more or less, its responsibility ends... Once an application for asylum has been accepted, refugees enter a formal, two-year integration programme, which includes language lessons and a reliable income

150,000 'good people': Marja Grill, Carolina Jemsby and Kenneth Ulander, 'Dubbelt så många gode män än tidigare trott', svt.se, 9 January 2017

An absence of official statistics on ethnicity and crime... Lee Roden, 'Why Sweden doesn't keep stats on ethnicity and crime', thelocal.se, 8 May 2018

That *Daily Mail* story: Nick Fagge, 'EXCLUSIVE – The city destroyed by migration: Inside the Swedish town where armed gangs patrol the streets, crime has exploded and a beautiful social worker's murder has shocked Europe', dailymail.co.uk, 30 January 2016

I found people struggling to cope... David Crouch, 'Gothenburg's refugee youths: "Come and meet us – nobody is here to be violent"', theguardian.com, 7 April 2016

A spate of deadly, gang-related violence... David Crouch, 'Sweden shooting puts focus on life in "ghettoes without hope"', theguardian.com, 20 March 2015

More than 500 days to get a decision on asylum: 'Avgjorda asyläренден beslutade av Migrationsverket, förstagångsansökningar, 2018', migrationsverket.se, 1 May 2018

The government cut its borrowing and debt fell... 'Stort budgetöverskott 2017', riksgalden.se, 9 January 2018

Joakim Ruist's estimates: Joakim Ruist, *Tid för Integration: Rapport till Expertgruppen för studier i offentlig ekonomi 2018:3*, Regeringskansliet, Finansdepartementet, 2018

Trust in Sweden's institutions appears to be rising... 'Resultat från SOM-seminariet 2018', som.gu.se, 25 April 2018

Andreas Johansson Heinö, 'Flyktingarna orsakade inte någon tillitskollaps', bt.se, 29 April 2018

Many of those who argue for tight limits on immigration... The locus classicus is David Goodhart's 2004 article 'Discomfort of strangers', reprinted on theguardian.com, 24 February 2004

500,000 new staff over the next 10 years... *Sveriges viktigaste jobb finns i välfärden: Rekryteringsrapport 2018*, Sveriges Kommuner och Landsting, Stockholm, 2018

The Gunnar Myrdal quote is from the condensed version of his 1,500-page report, published as *The Negro in America*, first issued in 1948. My edition was published in 1964 by Harper Torchbooks, New York, and the quote is on pages 318–319

Chapter 21: Empire

Books on the Wallenberg family include Ronald Fagerfjäll, 'To Move From The Old To What Is About To Come Is The Only Tradition Worth Keeping', Investor, Stockholm, 2016; and David Bartal, *The Empire: The Rise of the House of Wallenberg*, Dagens Industry, Stockholm, 1996

'We work our butts off in the financial part...' Interviewed by Richard Milne, 'The Wallenbergs: where money meets Swedish science', FT.com, 14 February 2017

Chapter 24: Reptilian

'We have taken a step into the premium league...' Quoted in Peter Campbell, 'Volvo Cars' profits driven by demand for SUVs', FT.com, 4 May 2016

On Clotaire Rapaille see, for example: Olle Hagman and Martin Bae Pedersen, 'How Big Became Bad: The Breakthrough and Stigmatization of "City Jeeps" in Sweden, 1984–2007', ICON, 16 (2010): 143–158

Stephen Graham, *Cities under Siege: The New Urban Militarism*, London, Verso, 2011

Chapter 25: Yank tank

Links to much of the material about the Asphalt Indians is still present on their defunct website: https://asfaltsdjungelnsindianer.wordpress.com/

They wrote in a popular newspaper... Asfaltsdjungelns indianer, 'Ditt lyxåk kör miljön i botten', aftonbladet.se, 13 August 2007

'The target has been to find a design that is not as "macho" as that of many other SUV models...' The quote is in: 'Volvo ACC concept car – first-class SUV challenger', media.volvocars.com, 8 January 1997

SUVs were intrinsically 'dangerous, thirsty and heavy'... Alla Bilar 2003 magazine, quoted in Hagman and Pedersen, as above

Sweden's fleet of cars was 'worst in class'... Per Kågeson, 'Reducing CO2 Emissions from New Cars: A progress report on the car industry's voluntary agreement and an assessment of the need for policy instruments', European Federation for Transport and Environment, Brussels, 2005

Chapter 26: National treasure

'Please let me try. It is my dream....' Quoted in 'Li Shufu', chinadaily. com.cn, 27 March 2006

Volvo could give him the innovation, branding and technology he needed... Pedro Nueno and Gary Liu, 'How Geely waited for Volvo', FT.com, 19 December 2011

Like 'a world famous movie star marrying a peasant in China'... As above

'The Chinese car industry is primitive...' Jacques Wallner, 'Kineserna har inget att lära Saab och Volvo', dn.se, 9 September 2009

'Geely can kill Volvo's strengths...' Lasse Swärd, 'Geely kan döda Volvos styrkor', dn.se, 5 December 2009

Sundemo: jobs will move out of Sweden... 'Geelys intresse väcker oro', svd.se, 9 September 2009

Unlisted companies in the Caymans... 'Facket vill att Geely ska granskas', dn.se, 9 December 2009

Sören Gyll quote: 'Gyll kämpar för Volvo PV', GP.se, 27 September 2009

Löfven's quotes on Geely: 'Svenska budgivare ger inte upp', GP.se, 28 October 2009

Li Shufu, 'Geely is Geely and Volvo is Volvo...' 'Li Shufu, CV and Biography', media.volvocars.com, 15 July 2010

Li Shufu, 'We gave them back their freedom'. Quoted in Richard Milne and Christian Shepherd, 'Volvo: Remaking the marque', FT.com, 19 June 2016

Chapter 27: Freeing the tiger

'In 2010, it took Volvo 44 months to develop a new car...'
Christer Karlsson is quoted as above

Gyllenhammar quotes: Karin Olander, 'Jag tycker att man har förstört hela Volvo', weekend.di.se, 14 July 2016

'The feeling among senior Volvo executives...' Jessica Twentyman, 'Volvo's digital launch of the XC90 marks "connected car" era', FT.com, 8 December 2015

Li Shufu, 'too Scandinavian': quoted in Milne and Shepherd, see above

Chapter 28: Toxic

On NOAH's plans for Brevik: 'NOAH vurderer videre farlig avfall-savfallsbehandling på Langøya etter at deponiet er fullt', noah. no, 17 September 2017

At the time this book went to print, the debate was still in full swing... See my piece for the *Financial Times*, 'Nordics tackle "Achilles heel" of incineration power schemes', ft.com, 12 March 2019

On the potential risks to local residents: Øyvind Lie, 'Planlegger gigantisk deponi for farlig avfall et steinkast unna boligområde', tu.no, 21 October 2015

James Corden's December 2016 broadcast is here: https://www. youtube.com/watch?v=t12bets0ABU

'If there's a paradise for environmentalists...' Gwladys Fouché, 'Sweden's carbon-tax solution to climate change puts it top of the green list', theguardian.com, 29 April 2008

More than half the energy Sweden generates is from renewable sources... says the official website of Sweden, sweden.se/quick-facts

Facebook consumes more than 1 per cent of Sweden's total energy production, a proportion set to double... 'Facebook effect turns Swedish steel town into tech hot-spot', af.reuters.com, 7 May 2018

On the 1972 UN environment conference in Stockholm: Richard Black, 'Stockholm: Birth of the green generation', bbc.com, 4 June 2012

Greenhouse gas emissions cut by a quarter while the economy has grown 60 per cent: 'When It Comes to Emissions, Sweden Has Its Cake and Eats It Too', worldbank.org, 16 May 2016

The tax on nitrogen oxide emissions: Lena Höglund-Isaksson and Thomas Sterner, 'Innovation Effects of the Swedish NOX Charge', OECD Global forum on Eco-innovation, Paris, 4–5 November 2009

Chapter 29: Goals

Sweden's climate agreement breaks the pattern of short-termism... Anders Wijkman, 'Historiskt klimatbeslut', hagainitiativet.se, 15 June 2017

Wijkman's quote 'Since the 1980s, capitalism has moved from furthering...' is from Ernst Ulrich von Weizsäcker and Anders Wijkman, Come On! Capitalism, Short-termism, Population and the Destruction of the Planet: A Report to the Club of Rome, Springer, New York, 2018, page 2

Short-term incentives are needed to reward long-term action... As above, page 96

The history of district heating in Sweden: Bengt Johansson *et al.*, *The Use of Biomass for Energy in Sweden: Critical Factors and Lessons Learned*, Report 35, Lund University Department of Energy and Environmental System Studies, 2002

Sweden's Climate Act: Akshat Rathi, 'Sweden legally commits to reaching net-zero emissions by 2045', qz.com, 16 June 2017

Chapter 30: Green shoots

'More world-leading tech companies than it should do...' According to a 2015 study by Atomico and Slush: *The State of European Tech*. Some more up-to-date gushing about Sweden's 'unicorn factory' can be found here: Chris O'Brien, 'Beyond Spotify and iZettle: How Sweden became Europe's capital of startup exits', venturebeat.com, 7 September 2018

Paris, Rome, London... Murad Ahmed, 'Stockholm: the unicorn factory', FT.com, 31 March 2015

'The orthodox view...' is expressed by Ben Chapman, 'How Sweden became one of the most innovative countries on earth', independent.co.uk, 8 August 2018

For the impact of the Home PC reform in Sweden, see '4 miljarder notan för hem-pc-reformen', computersweden.idg.se, 8 February 2002

Sebastian Siemiatkowski is quoted by Mac Bennell, 'Stockholm is rivalling Silicon Valley with a hotbed of technology start-ups', independent.co.uk, 17 December, 2014

De Greer is quoted by Liam Tung, 'Is Sweden the best place to start your start-up?', zdnet.com, 14 November 2012

Hjalmar Winbladh is quoted by Peter Cohan, 'After Skype, King, Mojang And Spotify; Here's What's Next From Stockholm', Forbes.com, 17 August 2017

Entrepreneurship in Sweden: Erik Stam and Mikael Stenkula, 'Intrapreneurship in Sweden: an international perspective', FIRES working paper, 2017

The importance of trust in innovation is pointed out by Alana Semuels, 'Why Does Sweden Have So Many Start-Ups?', theatlantic.com, 28 September 2017

Stenbeck's role is also mentioned by Ryan Darnell and Matt Weinberg, 'Sweden: Europe's Historic, Current And Future Innovation Hub', forbes.com, 19 April 2019

Conclusion

'What these groups see say more about them than about Sweden' – Johan Norberg 'The truth about Sweden: It's neither a Socialist paradise nor an Islamist horror movie', www.nydailynews.com, 5 March 2019

The term 'new Swedish model' has been around for a while. For example: Dimitris Tsarouhas, *Social Democracy in Sweden: The Threat from a Globalised World*, I. B. Tauris, 2008

When asked what the Swedish model stood for in 2012... Demoskop, 'Den svenska välfärden: Allmänhetens om framtida utmaningarna och möjligheterna', presented at Almedalen, 5 July 2012

'Sweden is proof that regulated capitalism...' This observation has been made eloquently by the eminent Swedish political scientist Bo Rothstein: 'Politikens höger-vänster har börjat spela ut sin roll', dn.se, 20 May 2017

Hybrit is a collaboration between private Swedish steel company SSAB, publicly owned iron ore miner LKAB, and public utility Vattenfall, backed by the state in the shape of the Swedish Energy Agency, Energimyndigheten

The current French president who has proposed a 'third way'... The experience of Macron in power suggests that he leans to the right in his economic preferences

That *Economist* special report: Adrian Wooldridge, 'The next super-model: politicians from both right and left could learn from the Nordic countries', special report on the Nordic countries, *The Economist*, 2 February 2013

Index